SPIRITUAL WEAPONS HANDBOOK

SPIRITUAL WEAPONS HANDBOOK

GAIL WINTER

Whitaker House

Publisher's Note:
Certain words and phrases have been printed in boldface type and/or italicized for emphasis by the author. However, the content of the verses remains unchanged.
Take note that the name "satan" is not capitalized, to indicate the author's choice not to acknowledge him, even to the point of violating grammatical rules.
Some quotations have been paraphrased.

Unless otherwise indicated, all Scripture quotations are taken from the *New King James Version*, © 1979, 1980, 1982, 1984 by Thomas Nelson, Inc. Used by permission. All rights reserved. Scripture quotations marked (AMP) are taken from the *Amplified® Bible*, © 1954, 1958, 1962, 1964, 1965, 1987 by The Lockman Foundation. Used by permission. (www.Lockman.org). Scripture quotations marked (CEV) are taken from the Holy Bible, *Contemporary English Version*, © 1991, 1992, 1995 by the American Bible Society. Used by permission. Scripture quotations marked (ESV) are taken from *The Holy Bible, English Standard Version*, © 2000, 2001, 1995 by Crossway Bibles, a division of Good News Publishers. Used by permission. All rights reserved. Scripture quotations marked (KJV) are taken from the King James Version of the Holy Bible. Scripture quotations marked (MSG) are taken from *The Message: The Bible in Contemporary Language* by Eugene H. Peterson, © 1993, 1994, 1995, 1996, 2000, 2001, 2002. Used by permission of NavPress Publishing Group. All rights reserved. Scripture quotations marked (NIV) are from the *Holy Bible, New International Version®, NIV®*, © 1973, 1978, 1984 by the International Bible Society. Used by permission of Zondervan. All rights reserved. Scripture quotations marked (NLT) are taken from the *Holy Bible, New Living Translation*, © 1996, 2004, 2007. Used by permission of Tyndale House Publishers, Inc., Carol Stream, Illinois 60188. All rights reserved. Scripture quotations marked (NIrV) are taken from the *Holy Bible, New International Reader's Version®, NIrV®*, © 1996, 1998 by Biblica. All rights reserved throughout the world. Used by permission of Biblica. Scripture quotations marked (GW) are taken from *God's Word®*, © 1995 by God's Word to the Nations. Used by permission of Baker Publishing Group.

Definitions of Hebrew and Greek words are taken from the electronic version of *Strong's Exhaustive Concordance of the Bible*, Strong's, (© 1980, 1986, and assigned to World Bible Publishers, Inc. Used by permission. All rights reserved.).

Spiritual Weapons Handbook:
A Collection of Prayers, Declarations, and Teachings to Blast the Devil

Speak His Word Ministries
www.speakhiswordministries.com
gail@speakhiswordministries.com

ISBN: 978-1-60374-889-6 • eBook ISBN: 978-1-60374-890-2
Printed in the United States of America
© 2010, 2013 by Gail Winter

Whitaker House
1030 Hunt Valley Circle
New Kensington, PA 15068
www.whitakerhouse.com

No part of this book may be reproduced or transmitted in any form or by any means, electronic or mechanical—including photocopying, recording, or by any information storage and retrieval system—without permission in writing from the publisher. Please direct your inquiries to permissionseditor@whitakerhouse.com.

2 3 4 5 6 7 8 9 10 11 12 13 **UJ** 22 21 20 19 18 17 16 15 14

DEDICATION

First and foremost, I dedicate this book to my Lord and Savior, Jesus Christ. Without Him I would be nothing; with Him I am everything He says I am! I can do everything He says I can do; I have what He says I can have!

I am so thankful that Jesus paid my debt, and that *"God would count [me] worthy of this calling, and fulfill all the good pleasure of His goodness, and the work of faith with power, that the name of our Lord Jesus Christ may be glorified in [me], and [I] in Him, according to the grace of our God, and the Lord Jesus Christ"* (2 Thessalonians 1:11–12).

I am deeply humbled by the calling that Father God placed upon my life to write and teach. He patiently led me on a journey that helped me identify and develop these gifts. I will forever be in awe of how He orchestrated so many divine connections and God-ordained relationships to encourage and assist me in this project. I am eternally grateful for the presence of the Holy Spirit, who constantly *"leads [me] by the way [I] should go"* (Isaiah 48:17).

I also dedicate this work to my precious family, who have allowed me to practice on them for the past thirty years. I thank God that He gave me Raymond as my husband to walk beside me on this journey. I am equally thankful that Raymond's primary spiritual gift is mercy!

We praise and glorify God every day that all of our children and their spouses love and serve the Lord. We are so proud of our daughter, Samarah, her husband, Michael, and our sons: Adair and his wife, Mysti; and Tag and his wife, Sarah. They have been patient, supportive, and willing to help me with anything I needed to complete this work. Our first and only grandchild so far, Natili Elisabeth, is our joy and delight. We declare that God's hand of blessing will be upon her always.

ACKNOWLEDGMENTS

I wish to express my utmost appreciation to Brother Don Gossett of Bold Bible Ministries, for his direction and for recommending I have this work published. In the many phone conversations I had with Brother Gossett, he always encouraged me to stay focused on fulfilling God's purpose for my life. He believed in me and in this work, even when I had only a tiny dream of spreading the message of this book. Without his encouragement, I never would have had the courage to contact Whitaker House Publishers.

Deepest, heartfelt thanks go to Haroletta Couch, who has been my friend, prayer partner, and proofreader since 2008, when I began self-publishing. She has spent untold hours helping me prepare this work for publication. Her attention to detail in proofreading is phenomenal, and my appreciation for her support of this vision is beyond words.

I also wish to acknowledge Janice Smith and Vicki Munoz for their passion in editing and critiquing the manuscript. God brought all three of us together through the most incredible set of circumstances, which resulted in us working together on this project. Janice's expertise in the Word, and Vicki's proficiency in grammar and composition, is a powerful combination that any author would envy. Because of this handbook, I now am honored to call them my sisters in the Lord.

My dear friend Peggy Kirchoff, author of *Why Sit Here Till We Die: Discovering Life in God's Word* (MileStones International

Publishers, 2005), told me more than twenty-five years ago that I should write books and curriculum. She has been a constant friend and prayer partner all these years; we have a kindred spirit that I have not seen equaled anywhere.

I would also like to thank Nancy James, author of *Destined to Triumph* (Triumph Ministries, 2005), for speaking into my life and supporting me in this endeavor. Her example of consistently living the "word of faith" message has raised the standard for those whom she touches.

In addition, I would like to thank some of the individuals who unknowingly have spoken into my life over the last thirty-five years. Their influence has been instrumental in helping develop these teachings and faith declarations. Primarily, these people include Don Gossett, Charles Capps, Kenneth and Gloria Copeland, Billye Brim, Jerry Savelle, Creflo Dollar, John Osteen, and Kenneth E. Hagin.

Brother Oral Roberts was one of the first people who taught us the miracle of seed-faith and how it works to meet any need. I will be forever grateful for the impact he made on our lives.

Finally, I would like to express my sincerest appreciation to my pastor, Dwight Kirskey of Celebration Family Church. His love and support mean the world to me! I can always count on him to give a word of encouragement. Thank you for all you do, Pastor K.

—*Gail Winter*

CONTENTS

Preface 17
Introduction 18

Part I: Battle Preparations
Unleash the Power of Your Words 30
Develop a Passion for His Presence 36
Nuclear Weapons in a Nutshell 44

Part II: Nuclear Strategies to Blast the Devil
Declare Victory over the Flesh 48
    Prayer of Confession and Repentance 48
    Declarations of Freedom from Slavery to Sin 49
    Prayer of Victory over the Old Nature 50
    Prayer for Others with Addictions 52
    Declarations of Victory over Lust 53
    Prayer of Victory over the Flesh 55
Know Your Identity in Christ Jesus 60
    Confession of Who I Am, According to God 60
    Confession of Who I Am in Christ 62
    Bold Declarations of Anointing 65
Exercise Your Authority 66
    Declarations of Authority over the Devil 70
    Declarations of a Hedge of Protection 71

 The "Nuclear Bomb" of Binding 75
 Declarations of Loosing 76
 The "Nuclear Bomb" of Loosing 77
 Prayer of Binding and Loosing 85
 Commanding Declaration 87
 Commanding Prayer 88
 Declarations of Immunity 90
Overcome Adversity 92
 Mountain-Moving Declaration 101
 Mountain-Moving Confession 101
 Confessions of Breakthrough 103
Invoke the Blood of Jesus 107
 Declarations to Honor the Blood of Jesus 108
 Declarations to Activate the Blood of Jesus 109
 Declaration to Apply the Blood of Jesus 111
 Declaration to Hold and Sprinkle the Blood of Jesus 114
 Declaration to Draw a Blood Line 115
 Additional Declarations to Apply, Plead, and Otherwise
  Activate the Blood 116
Declare the Blessing 119
 Scriptural Assurances of God's Blessing for the Family 120
 Declarations of God's Blessing for the Family 120
 Declarations of God's Blessing for Children 121
 Prayer for a Teenager 124
 Declarations of Prosperity and Provision 125
 Declarations of Divine Blessing, Favor, and Guidance 127
 Declarations of Divine Wisdom, Knowledge,
  and Success 129
 Declarations of Righteousness 130

    Declarations of Blessings Based on Deuteronomy 28........131
    Scriptural Declarations of Blessings..................................... 132
    Declarations to Release the Blessing into
        Every Part of Our Being...133

Trust in God's Faithfulness 135
    Scriptural Declarations of Trust in God 135
    Declaration of Trust in God... 136
    Scriptural Confessions of God's Faithfulness 137

Part III: Topical Guide to Biblical Confessions, Declarations, and Prayers

A Church or Ministry..142
    Declarations of Fruitful Ministry and
        Widespread Salvation...142
    Prayer for Pastors and Ministry Leaders 145
    Declarations for Pastors and Ministry Leaders 145

Comfort in Times of Grief and Sadness 147
    Prayer for Comfort After Loss of Loved One 149
    Scriptures to Stand On After Loss of Loved One...............149
    Scriptures of Assurance of God's Presence 150
    Prayer to Combat Loneliness 151
    Declarations of Joy and Contentment 152
    Declarations of Peace...153

Employment 156
    Prayer for a New Job... 156
    Confession for a New Job... 157
    Prayer for Favor on the Job 158
    Declaration of Increase... 159
    Scriptural Declarations of Prosperity 160

Favor 163
    Confessions of Favor 165
Fear/Worry 167
    Confessions of Freedom from Fear and Anxiety 167
    Confessions of Faith Rather than Fear 168
    Scripture to Stand On in the Face of Fear 169
    Anti-Anxiety Confessions 170
    Declarations for Stress Management 171
    Declarations of Abundant Material Provision 173
    Prayer of Binding and Loosing of Finances 176
    Scriptural Declaration of Blessings in Any Economy 177
    Prayer for Financial Breakthrough 178
    Scriptural Confessions to Combat Worry 181
Forgiveness 184
    Prayer of Forgiveness 186
    Prayer of Commitment to Walk in Forgiveness 188
    Declaration of Forgiveness 189
Health/Healing 190
    Scriptural Confessions of Healing 191
    Declaration to Stop Bleeding 198
    Declaration to Repel Recurring Symptoms 199
    Confession in Preparation for Communion 200
    Declaration of Healing (Communion) 200
    Prayer to Affirm Faith for Healing 201
    Declarations of Faith for Health 203
    Declarations to Command the Body 205
    Prayer to Seal Your Healing 205
Love/Marriage 206

- Prayer to Live in Love 206
- Declarations of Love 207
- Prayer of Commitment to Love..................................... 208
- Confession for a Harmonious Marriage 209
- Prayer for a Harmonious Marriage 210
- Prayer to Defeat the Spirit of Divorce.............................211

Personal Edification 212
- Declarations to Build Up Your Inner Man 212
- Declarations to Frame Your Future................................. 213
- Declarations to Edify Your Spirit-Man 215
- Declarations to Establish God's Word in Your Life..........216
- Declarations to Establish Yourself in Righteousness 217
- My "Never Again" List 219
- Positive, Faith-Filled Confessions I 223
- Confessions of Success 224
- Positive, Faith-Filled Confessions II............................... 228
- Scriptures to Cast Off Fear and Unbelief 229
- Prayer to Cast Off Fear and Unbelief............................. 230

Prayer 231
- Petition for a Heavenly Grant 233
- General Intercessory Declarations 235
- Prayer for Nation and Leaders....................................... 239
- Declaratory Prayer for the Security of the United States. 240
- Prayer for Jerusalem 241
- Prayer of Thanksgiving 241
- Confessions of a Life Pleasing to God 242

Protection 245
- Prayer for Protection I.. 245

    Prayer for Protection II 246
    Prayer for Putting On the Armor of God 247
    Declaration of Protection Based on Psalm 91 249
Salvation and Spiritual Growth 250
    Scriptures of Salvation 250
    Personal Salvation Prayer 251
    Scriptural Assurances of Salvation for Family Members .. 252
    Declarations of Salvation for Others 252
    Prayer of Repentance 254
    Tither's Confession 255
    Prayer of Provision Based on Malachi 3:8–12 255
    Prayer to Anoint an Offering 256
    Prayer for Spiritual Growth 257
    Prayer for Baptism in the Holy Spirit 260
Sowing and Reaping 263
    Seeds to Sow if You Want to Reap...
    Healing 264
    Abundant Provision 264
    Miracles 265
    Divine Direction and Guidance 266
    Boldness Instead of Fear 266
    The Peace of Protection and Safety 267
    Salvation, for Yourself or Others 268
    Victory over Weakness and Failure 269
    The Joy of Seeing Your Children and
       Grandchildren Serving God 270
Wisdom and Guidance 271
    Prayer for Guidance in Decision Making 271
    Prayer for Wisdom 272

- Declarations of Divine Wisdom and Guidance 273
- Scriptural Confessions of Knowing All Things 274

Worship 276
- Prayer to Bless the Names of God 276
- Psalm 23: A Guide for Praise and Worship Using the Redemptive Names of Jehovah 280
- Scriptures and Scriptural Declarations to Exalt the Lord 284

About the Author 287

PREFACE

Spiritual Weapons Handbook began as a handbook I compiled for use in ministering to others. Because I frequently pray for people concerning many areas of their lives, it became necessary to bring together the Scriptures and materials I used in a single resource for easy access when ministering to people.

As a teacher, I was continually giving out "confession cards" and other various materials in my classes. These tools were invaluable for teaching people how to overcome the adversities in their lives by speaking aloud and meditating on Scriptures and concepts from the Word of God. These people began asking for copies to give to their family and friends; and so, the next logical step was to make this material available to them in a user-friendly format.

Another consideration for publishing *Spiritual Weapons Handbook* was the need to teach people how to believe God for themselves. It does very little good for people to get healed if they do not know how to stay healed! And in order to stay healed, one has to learn to *think right* and *speak right*—all of the time!

When I minister to people, it is simply not feasible for me to spend two or three hours teaching them the principles of believing God and expecting things from Him. Nor is it feasible to attempt, in a short amount of time, to teach them their covenant rights as believers in order to build their faith to receive from God. Instead, I have made available this resource of Scriptures and Scripture-based declarations, so that the people to whom I minister may renew their minds and learn to think like God thinks, with the end result being the *continued manifestation* of the healing, victory, or other answer to prayer.

INTRODUCTION

When you were born again, you were literally born into a royal family. The King of Kings and Lord of Lords adopted you into His family, and now you can enjoy all the rights and privileges associated with royalty. You now have access to a royal inheritance! Would you like to know how to receive and enjoy that inheritance? Let me show you!

Affirming God's Word sincerely, from the heart, will strengthen your faith and enable you to lay claim to your inheritance as a believer. If you affirm—that is, "re-speak"—God's Word each day, it will get into your spirit man; you will totally change your world! Knowing and trusting God's promises changes everything in our lives. We must believe that God cannot lie; that if He said it in His Word, it is ours—if we abide in Him and receive those promises by faith.

Spiritual Weapons Handbook is a collection of confessions, biblical affirmations, and scriptural principles to help intensify your faith, resulting in a wall of protection that the enemy cannot penetrate!

Even though this book is based on Scripture and includes many biblical references and paraphrases, it is not meant to replace your Bible but to complement it. You should study the whole counsel of the Word of God. Acts 17:11 admonishes us to examine the Scriptures to see if what we are being taught is true. Therefore, *Spiritual Weapons Handbook* should be used as a springboard for your own search for answers from the Word of God. Ideally, you should use a respected study Bible alongside this handbook to help you find additional Scriptures that speak to your need.

Spiritual Weapons Handbook should not be used as a ritual—a mere babbling of the Scriptures in an attempt to find a "magic formula." Much more important is your relationship with the Father and personal revelation from the Word of God.

YOU GET TO DECIDE!

This handbook is based on the premise that we, like God, can speak things into being. This truth comes across in the following Scriptures:

> *You will also declare a thing, and it will be established for you.* (Job 22:28)

> *God…calls those things which do not exist as though they did.* (Romans 4:17)

> *Declare what is to be….* (Isaiah 45:21 NIV)

> *I am God,…declaring the end from the beginning.* (Isaiah 46:9–10)

Like God, we are supposed to declare, call, and proclaim the things we desire, in accordance with the Word of God.

To further confirm the importance of speaking His Word, God says, "*My word, **which comes from my mouth**, is like the rain and snow. It will not come back to me without results. It will accomplish whatever I want and achieve whatever I send it to do*" (Isaiah 55:11 GW).

It is quite obvious that God thinks words are very important. Not only that; He places great importance on vocalizing—*speaking aloud*—His Word.

My objective is to teach you how to *"declare a thing"* and how to *"[call]…things which do not* [yet!] *exist"* until they are manifested. You will learn how to speak into existence the things you desire, and thereby determine your future! You will learn to say the way you want it *to be* rather than merely establish the way that it is according to your five physical senses at the present moment.

This handbook is designed to help born-again believers come into agreement with the Word of God and its application to their lives by confessing—that is, re-speaking—and meditating upon the Scriptures. As you meditate on God's Word, the reality of all that He wants to give you will saturate your soul and spirit. This will give you the confidence to believe and claim each promise in His Word as your own.

SPEAK THINGS INTO EXISTENCE

We speak things into existence through faith declarations. What is a faith declaration? A faith declaration is made when we speak God's Word out loud in faith. Someone once said that when you "pray" Scripture, to you it may sound like it is yourself simply praying, but to the devil, it sounds just like God speaking! The devil does not know differently *until* you open your mouth and say something that doesn't agree with God's Word. Then, the devil has your number and your location—that is, where you are spiritually! So, be wise, and speak only what God says!

These Scriptures confirm the importance of speaking the Word:

You shall return and obey the voice of the Lord and do all His commandments....This commandment which I command you this day is not too difficult for you, nor is it far off. It is not [a secret laid up] in heaven, that you should say, Who shall go up for us to heaven and bring it to us, that we may hear and do it? Neither is it beyond the sea, that you should say, Who shall go over the sea for us and bring it to us, that we may hear and do it? But the word is very near you, in your mouth and in your mind and in your heart, so that you can do it.
(Deuteronomy 30:8, 11–13 AMP)

For out of the fullness (the overflow, the superabundance) of the heart the mouth speaks. (Matthew 12:34 AMP)

This Book of the Law shall not depart out of your mouth, but you shall meditate on it day and night, that you may observe and do according to all that is written in it. For then you shall make your way prosperous, and then you shall deal wisely and have good success. (Joshua 1:8 AMP)

Yet we have the same spirit of faith as he had who wrote, I have believed, and therefore have I spoken. We too believe, and therefore we speak. (2 Corinthians 4:13 AMP)

In order to "work the Word," you must have:

1. *A relationship with the Father.* Jesus said, "If you live in me and what I say lives in you, then ask for anything you want, and it will be yours" (John 15:7 GW). That's relationship!

2. *Revelation from the Holy Spirit.* As you meditate on the Word, revelation of that Word comes from the Holy Spirit. Without revelation, the declarations will remain mere words on a page.

IT'S ALL ABOUT RELATIONSHIP!

The prayers and Scripture-based declarations in this book are not meant to be "shortcuts," nor do they replace a close and intimate relationship with Jesus Christ. In fact, having an intimate relationship with Father God is paramount to seeing our prayers answered and to living in victory.

Before you can effectively "blast the devil" out of your life, you must get to know God and seek to understand His great love for you. The apostle Paul was determined to get to know the Father intimately. He wrote,

> [For my determined purpose is] **that I may know Him** [that I may progressively become more deeply and intimately acquainted with Him,...that I may so share His sufferings as to be continually transformed [in spirit into His likeness even] to His death.   (Philippians 3:10 AMP)

Share in his determination. Fall in love with Jesus. Express your appreciation to the Holy Spirit for His presence and guidance. It really is all about relationship! Your purpose should be to seek His face, not His hand.

There may be times when you simply wish to sit there, not saying or doing anything except "beholding" Him—looking intently at His face in the Spirit and just being with Him. Then, at other times, you will need to pursue His presence. It is in these times that you will find this handbook very helpful.

The Word of God Renews Your Mind

It is not possible to overemphasize the importance of renewing the mind. As Creflo Dollar says, "There can be no spiritual growth without renewing the mind through the Word of God."[1] Neither will you ever overcome addictions and destructive behaviors without changing your way of thinking.

No frequency of the laying on of hands, no degree of deliverance, and no amount of willpower will make a bit of difference until you commit to becoming a disciple of the Lord Jesus Christ who has learned to think like He thinks. Once our thinking lines up with the Word of God, we find success in overcoming addictions and bad behaviors because we have *acted* on the Word that we know.

Beyond a shadow of a doubt, the mind is where the battle is. Your body does only what the mind tells it to do. One of the purposes of this handbook is to teach you how to renew your mind through the Word of God so that you and your loved ones may experience lasting change.

The Word of God Gives Way to Nuclear Prayers That Blast the Devil

When we pray—that is, "re-speak" the Word of God—we use weapons that produce a nuclear explosion in the kingdom of darkness. When we apply the blood of Jesus, we become radioactive to the devil! Declare your "safe perimeter"—the enemy will not be able to cross the blood line. The devil and his demons are very afraid of the blood of Jesus and the spoken Word of God, so be bold!

HOW TO USE THIS HANDBOOK

Part I of this handbook will establish some basic principles of the victorious Christian life, including our authority over the devil

---

1. Creflo Dollar, *How to Change Your Thinking* (audio teaching).

and our identity in Christ Jesus. This section is intended to equip you to engage in spiritual warfare and to tap into the power of your words in order to defeat the devil.

Part II gets more specific, introducing you to specific strategies that are effective for blasting the devil. You will learn how to exercise authority over all the power of the enemy and blast the devil out of your affairs! You never have to lose another battle to the devil.

Part III is a topical guide to nuclear strategies, arranged alphabetically, that address many of your needs. Find the topic(s) that relate to your particular battle, and use those biblical declarations to speak to your situation. When the pressures of life come knocking at your door, or come crashing in like a flood, you will have a concise compilation of Scriptures that will target your problem and keep you thinking straight.

I challenge you to read aloud from parts II and III every day for thirty consecutive days. Doing so will increase revelation knowledge of God's love and provision for every area of your life. Repeat the declarations out loud several times, reading them slowly as you meditate on them. Let the truth of God's Word sink deep into your heart. It will change you at the most profound level and will give you peace and faith to overcome every adverse situation.

Be consistent in your prayer time, but do not get in a rut. It is important, however, to begin each day by inviting the Holy Spirit to guide you and by worshipping and adoring the Father and Jesus. Likewise, it is important to daily apply the blood of protection over your family and loved ones—not out of fear but out of awareness that the devil's aim is *"to steal, to kill, and to destroy"* (John 10:10). You must be vehement in letting him know that you will not allow this!

Due Diligence

As in all successful ventures, diligence is a must. We must be diligent in confessing and meditating on the Word of God. Set aside time daily to confess the Scriptures aloud. This time of confessing the Word should be in addition to the time that is spent in worshipping God, reading the Word, and praying for specific needs.

Some days, you may be short on time when you go to make your biblical affirmations. When this is the case, refer directly to "Nuclear Weapons in a Nutshell" on page 44 and "Psalm 23: A Guide for Praise and Worship Using the Redemptive Names of Jehovah" on page 280. These declarations cover several vital points in just a sentence or two. Spend at least five minutes every day declaring who you are in Christ. Doing so will keep you grounded and will increase your confidence in the integrity of God's Word.

When you pray the Word of God, you are praying for the exact thing God desires. You never have to be concerned that you are praying anything outside of the will of God.

Personalize It

You must make these prayers and confessions your own. Repeatedly throughout this handbook, you will find the phrases "You can pray something like this" and "You can use this as a pattern." Use the *Spiritual Weapons Handbook* as a guide until you are familiar enough with the Scriptures to incorporate your own words.

The Bible was written to you! My desire is to show you how you can personalize the Scriptures for your particular needs. In most cases, I have used the pronouns *we*, *us*, and *our* because I always include all my family when I pray. You may wish to say *I*, *me*, and so forth, instead.

Get to Know the Will of God

Faith can begin only where the will of God is known! In other words, it is simply impossible to believe God for something that we are not fully convinced He wants us to have. For example, if we are not confident that God desires the sick to be healed *all of the time*, we cannot offer prayers for healing with any confidence that they will be answered.

Likewise, we cannot pray with any assurance that God will actually take care of our material needs if we do not understand that *"my God **shall** supply all your need [all of the time] according to His riches in glory by Christ Jesus"* (Philippians 4:19). For that reason, most of the topics covered in this handbook are accompanied by a short teaching to deepen your understanding of God's will.

Meditate

Biblical meditation must be based on the Word of God. Psalm 1:1–2 says, *"Blessed is the man...[whose] delight is in the law of the* Lord, *and **in His law he mediates** day and night."* The Hebrew word used for *"meditates"* is *hagah*, meaning "to reflect; to moan, to mutter; to ponder; to imagine; to contemplate something as one repeats the words."[2] Thus, true biblical meditation involves "re-speaking" Scriptures and biblical principles out loud, and then pondering and meditating on them. It is the process whereby the thoughts in our head become lodged in our heart—for good or for evil, I might add.

Biblical meditation is *not* the emptying of our minds, as taught in Eastern religions. Quite the opposite! Christian meditation involves *filling* our minds with the Word of God.

It is important that your effort not be halfhearted as you read the Scriptures and faith declarations. Rather, you should read

---

2. Strong's #H1897.

them aloud with sincerity and then meditate on each one. As you do this, the Word of God will get down into your spirit and will open your heart to receive revelation knowledge. Then, you will be able to speak His Word in faith without hesitation when trying situations arise in your life. It is better to read and meditate on only one or two Scriptures at a time than to read twenty chapters without receiving any revelation knowledge.

Build Your Wall

It is important to speak the Word every day as a preventative measure. Every time you speak the Word, it is like building a wall of protection around you and your loved ones—brick by brick, the wall rises, and with each brick you are better able to *"stand against the wiles of the devil"* (Ephesians 6:11).

Memorize at least one Scripture for every area of life so that you can speak the Word of God instantly in any given situation. Start with the "Positive, Faith-Filled Confessions I and II" on pages 223 and 228. Don't let crisis take you by surprise! You must be prepared *before* the storm arrives; otherwise, you will speak words of fear and doubt instead of faith. Your first words matter! The first words out of your mouth reveal what's in your heart (see Luke 6:45), and they will very likely determine the outcome of the situation.

Daily speaking the Word will cause you to be more sensitive and alert to the plans and schemes of the enemy—your adversary, the devil—who tries to find an open door to attack you and your loved ones. Declaring the Word of God with authority will stop the devil in his tracks before his attack becomes full-blown. This is how to build immunity to the attacks of the enemy, and it is the most effective use of biblical affirmations!

Final Authority

One of the most important faith principles you can learn is how to make the Word of God the final authority in your life. If you will determine to do that, you will find stability when everything else around you is turned upside-down. Let what God's Word says about your situation settle the matter. Only then will you be confident when others are confused, peaceful when others are falling apart, and victorious when others are caving in to pressures.

What does it mean to make God's Word the final authority? It means believing what God says instead of believing what other people say. It means believing what God says instead of what your circumstances scream. Make up your mind today to live by faith, not by sight. (See 2 Corinthians 5:7.) Fearlessly commit yourself to the authority of God's Word; that way, there will be nothing in this unstable world that can steal your security from you.

I pray that this *Spiritual Weapons Handbook* will bless you "*exceedingly abundantly above all that* [you] *can ask or think, according to the power of the Holy Spirit that works in* [you]" (Ephesians 3:20).

PART I:
BATTLE PREPARATIONS

UNLEASH THE POWER OF YOUR WORDS

Words have the power to create and to effect change. Did you know that there would have been no creation without spoken words? Genesis chapter 1 records how God created the world by using *words*. He did not create the universe by thinking about it. He did not create light by molding materials in His hands—there were no materials! "*God said, 'Let there be light'; and there was light*" (Genesis 1:3).

Genesis 1:2 states that the earth was dark and had no form; the Holy Spirit was hovering over the face of the waters, just waiting. "***Then*** *God said…*" (Genesis 1:3). Nothing happened, nothing changed, until God *said* something! Six times in the first chapter of Genesis, we read, "*God said,…and it was so*"! We have this confirmation in Hebrews 11:3: "*The worlds were framed by the word of God.*"

A PATTERN ESTABLISHED BY GOD

It is imperative to understand that when God wants to change something, He *speaks* to it. This is a huge clue as to how we can change our circumstances. If you want a life full of blessings, health, abundance, and joy, then you are going to have to follow God's pattern—His way of doing things.

Abraham, like God, spoke things into existence—he *"called those things that be not, as though they were"* (Romans 4:17). Just as light was "not yet" until God spoke it into existence, so the womb of Abraham's wife, Sarah, was not fruitful until Abraham got his mouth in line with God's Word. Calling himself "Abraham," or "father of a multitude" brought his mouth into agreement with God's promise to him. Every time someone called him by that name, he or she was also affirming the promise that Abraham would be the father of many nations.

Jesus Followed the Pattern

God used words to create and establish the universe, and then He taught Jesus to do the same. Jesus used words and commanded inanimate objects and nature to obey Him, and they did. Scripture tells us that the wind and waves calmed at Jesus' command (see Mark 4:39; Luke 8:25); likewise, a fig tree dried up from the roots at His command (see Mark 11:12–14, 20–23). So, we can see that creation responded to the words Jesus spoke. There appears to be a pattern emerging, and we would be wise to take heed of it.

> **YOUR WORDS HAVE AUTHORITY!**

Let's take a closer look at the story of the withered fig tree.

Now the next day, when they had come out from Bethany, He was hungry. And seeing from afar a fig tree having leaves, He went to see if perhaps He would find something on it. When He came to it, He found nothing but leaves, for it was not the season for figs. In response Jesus said to it, "Let no one eat fruit from you ever again." And His disciples heard it....Now in the morning, as they passed by, they saw the fig tree dried up from the roots. (Mark 11:12–14, 20)

Doesn't that sound a lot like *"And God said…and it was so"*?

Now, remember—Jesus spoke and did only what His Father taught Him to. (See, for example, John 5:19.) He *expected* results— He *expected* that tree to change! He was not a bit surprised that it was dead! Jesus had faith in His own words; He had confidence that when He spoke to the tree, *it had to change*! We must acquire that same confidence in the creative power of our words.

Jesus Passed On the Pattern to His Disciples

The disciples were shocked that the tree was completely dead, so Jesus took the opportunity to teach them. First, He taught them that they must use the same kind of faith that God uses. (See Mark 11:22.) Then, He continued instructing them, telling them that the God-kind of faith *speaks!* (See Mark 11:23–24.)

Jesus taught the disciples that they, too, could change things. Jesus did not say, "Well now, I'm the only one who can speak to things and cause them to change. You know, I *am* the Son of God!" No! He taught them that they, too, could *speak* the desired outcome and bring it to pass. For example, He said, *"If **you** have faith as a mustard seed, you can **say**…"* (Luke 17:6).

FAITH SPEAKS

Faith always speaks! We see that this basic principle is absolutely essential to being spiritually born again. According to Romans 10:8–10, the way to be saved is by confessing with our mouths as well as believing in our hearts. This process applies to everything we need from God. The literal meaning of the Greek terms for *"saved"* (*sozo*) and *"salvation"* (*soteria*) in this passage includes not only eternal life but also deliverance, rescue, protection, health and healing, and prosperity.[34]

So, you see, if you will *believe* and *speak*, it will happen for you, also! You must have faith in *your* words! You must have faith that what you say will come to pass.

Now, lest you say in your heart, "Yes, but that was God! Yes, but that was Jesus! Yes, but those were the disciples who walked with Jesus," let me remind you of something else Jesus said: *"Most assuredly, I say to you, He who believes on Me, the works that I do he will do also; and greater works than these he will do, because I go to My Father"* (John 14:12).

God has given us the same authority and the same ability to change things as He did Jesus. We, too, can control and remove anything that stands in the way of the will of God. Ephesians 5:1 tells us to *"be imitators of God."* Likewise, God said in Genesis 1:26–28, *"Let Us [the Trinity] make man in Our image, according to Our likeness."* The Hebrew words for *"image"*[5] and *"likeness"*[6] means "to resemble," or "in the same manner." Is it a stretch to say that we are supposed to be like God? No!

Talk to Your Mountain

What is it you want? What is it you need? You get to decide the way it will be! Find God's promise to you for your situation, and speak it to your mountain—it will be!

A mountain is symbolic of an obstacle, hindrance, or insurmountable problem. What is your mountain? It may be sickness. It may be a troublesome relationship. It may be a lack of money. Do not pray *about* the mountain. Do not talk *about* the mountain.

---

3. Strong's #G4982.
4. Strong's #G4991.
5. Strong's #H6754.
6. Strong's #H1823.

Instead, speak *to* the mountain. If you really want answers to your prayers, you must speak to the situation, as impossible as it may seem. Do not use your words to describe your present condition or situation. Use faith-filled words to create your desired outcome.

God's method of creating and changing is to *speak*, and our method should be same! God's Word alone, printed on the pages of a book, will do nothing for you. This fact may shock you, but merely reading the Word of God has relatively little power. It is when we *speak* the Word of God out of our mouths that we will see strongholds broken off our lives, and our screwed-up ways of thinking corrected. We must pick up God's Word and start "re-speaking" the Scriptures out of our mouths if we are really serious about changing the world around us and getting our prayers answered.

Speak Up—Your Life Is at Stake![7]

There are principles in the Word of God that are imperative for you to understand because your life and the lives of your loved ones truly are at stake. We are in a great spiritual war. We simply cannot afford to be lackadaisical in using the weapons God has made available to us. If we remain apathetic, the devil will most surely chew us up and spit us out! If you have been experiencing one crisis after another, the reason may be apathy.

In order to beat the devil at his game, we must follow the pattern God established for doing things. In 2 Corinthians 4:13–14, the apostle Paul, inspired by the Holy Spirit, wrote, *"Since we have the same spirit of faith* [The same as who? Jesus!], *according to what is written, 'I believed and therefore I spoke'; we also believe and therefore speak"* (2 Corinthians 4:13–14). We, too, must speak what we believe.

---

[7]. Inspired by Don Gossett's radio broadcast series *Speak Up! Your Life Is at Stake!*

As Paul endured hardships and even the possibility of death, he was following the pattern of the psalmist as expressed in Psalm 116. He had learned that, even in the midst of perils, he could experience the life of Jesus by speaking out the Word he believed. He had learned that *speaking* releases the resources of heaven into the situation.

Not only do you speak once you believe, but *speaking* will help you to *believe*! Does not the Scripture say, *"Faith comes by hearing, and hearing by the word of God"* (Romans 10:17)? So, if you need "bigger faith," you need to hear more of the Word. As you speak the Word of God out loud, your ears hear it, causing your confidence in the Word to grow. God makes this so easy for us! Faith is not hard, as long as we follow His pattern.

NOT FOR EVERY BELIEVER

"What?" you say. "I thought all of God's promises were for every believer!" Nope! Consider again what Jesus said in Mark 11:22–23 (KJV): *"Have faith in God.* [The *Basic English Bible* translates this phrase as *"Have God's faith."*] *For verily I say unto you, That* **whosoever shall say** *unto this mountain, Be thou removed, and be thou cast into the sea;…he shall have whatsoever he saith."*

The promise here is not for everyone—no, indeed! It is for *"whoever shall* **say**"!

DEVELOP A PASSION FOR HIS PRESENCE

Daily we must recognize our intense need for the presence of the Lord Jesus Christ in our lives. As the lease on this planet earth is about to expire, the dark is becoming darker; the light is becoming lighter. There will no longer be a gray area of compromise and indecision. To not only survive but thrive in this *"present evil world"* (Galatians 1:4 KJV), you must be *turned inside out* for Him.

There may be no greater example of a hunger for the presence of God than what David portrayed in Psalms 27 and 63. The passages below adeptly describe a passion to *live* in His presence—to experience a face-to-face encounter with Him every day.

> There is *one thing* that I have sought God for—*one thing* that I desperately desire more than anything else—and that is to live and remain *in His presence* every moment of my life, delighting in the Lord's perfections and meditating on His faithfulness. (Psalm 27:4–5, author's paraphrase)

> O God, You are my God; I earnestly search for You. My soul thirsts for You; my whole body longs for You. *In Your presence* I experience Your power and glory. Your unfailing love is better to me than life itself. O how I praise You! (Psalm 63:1–2, author's paraphrase)

David wrote Psalm 63 when he was in the wilderness, feeling weak and exhausted. Even so, he declared his need for *El*, "the strong One," which was especially fitting, since David needed mental and physical strength.

The prophet Jeremiah said of the Lord, *"His word was in my heart like a burning fire shut up in my bones; I was weary of holding it back, and I could not"* (Jeremiah 20:9).

If I could bestow on you one gift, it would be a passion for God, a hunger for His presence, an insatiable thirst for His Word. *Passion* can be defined as a powerful and compelling emotion that cannot be easily squelched.

The following section will take you through a process that will help you become more *"intimately acquainted with Him"* (Philippians 3:10 AMP). You will learn how to use Scriptures to express your love for the Lord.

STEPS TO INTIMACY

1. *Draw Near to God*

Draw near to God and He will draw near to you.
(James 4:8)

When you draw near to God, He promises to draw near to you. This act of drawing closer to Him conveys a sense of urgency to be near Him, to experience a sense of intimacy with Him. As an act of your will, you make a deliberate decision to move closer to Him in the Spirit. This step has nothing to do with feelings. God is worthy of all of our praise, no matter how we feel or what we are going through.

Every person must choose for himself how closely he will follow Jesus and how intimate his walk with Him will be. God is completely accessible to every person who is willing to surrender to Him.

You could pray something like this: "Precious heavenly Father, I long for intimacy with You. I want to know You more deeply and intimately, and to be continually transformed into Your image. I long to see Your face and to hear Your voice; I long to know the mysteries and secrets that can be learned only in Your presence. Draw me close to You, Lord. Amen."

2. Purposely Pursue His Presence

When You [God] said, "Seek My face," my heart said to You, "Your face, LORD, I will seek." (Psalm 27:8)

We must deliberately pursue the presence of God. As we speak out Scriptures like these below, we will find ourselves longing for God's presence more and more. By faith, we declare our desire for Him, which invites fellowship with His Spirit.

My soul longs, yes, even faints for the courts of the LORD [His presence]; my heart and my flesh cry out for the living God. (Psalm 84:2)

Truly my soul silently waits for God; from Him comes my salvation....My soul, wait silently for God alone, for my expectation is from Him. (Psalm 62:1, 5)

3. Magnify the Lord

And Mary said: "My soul magnifies the Lord." (Luke 1:46)

Insert your name in the Scripture above; make it personal. Again, loving and worshipping God is an act of our will, not our feelings!

We will discuss the worship of God in greater detail later on in this chapter. For now, you could pray something like this:

Heavenly Father, I worship and adore You because You are great and You are greatly to be praised. (See Psalm 48:1.) You are my God forever, and You will be my Guide, even unto death. (See Psalm 48:14.) You are worthy, O Lord, to receive glory, honor, adoration, and power, because You have created all things, and You created all things for Your pleasure. (See Revelation 4:11.) You truly are the King of Kings and the Lord of Lords, and I will honor, adore, and serve You throughout my life.

4. Confess and Repent of Sin

Cleanse your hands, you sinners; and purify your hearts, you double-minded. (James 4:8)

Confess your trespasses to one another, and pray for one another, that you may be healed. The effective, fervent prayer of a righteous man avails much. (James 5:16)

Effective prayer involves repentance and is an important part of intimacy.

You could say something like this: "Holy Spirit, I ask You to reveal to me any unconfessed sin I might have in my heart. Father God, I repent of all wrong motives, attitudes, and actions. Father, thank You for the precious sacrifice Jesus endured for me. Thank You for the blood of Jesus, which cleanses me from all unrighteousness. I receive Your forgiveness by faith in the name of Jesus. Now, Lord, I forgive anyone who has offended me. I loose that person and let him go free. In Jesus' name I pray, amen."

5. Commit to Kingdom Priorities

The kingdom of God is…righteousness and peace and joy in the Holy Spirit. (Romans 14:17)

But the fruit of the Spirit is love, joy, peace, longsuffering, kindness, goodness, faithfulness, gentleness, self-control. Against such there is no law. (Galatians 5:22–23)

The fruit of the Spirit is evidence of the Word in us. If we are not demonstrating this fruit as we should, then we do not really have the Word in us to the extent that we should. We should always use the fruit of the Spirit as our measuring stick to determine if we really are doers of the Word and not hearers only. (See James 1:22.)

Pray, "Father God, I declare that Your righteousness, joy, and peace are established in my life. I do not walk in my own righteousness but in Your righteousness, by the blood of Jesus. I thank You, Father, that great is my peace and undisturbed composure. (See Isaiah 54:13.) I set my will to walk in love and forgiveness. Thank You for sharing Your kingdom, power, and glory with me. (See Matthew 6:9–13.) In Jesus' name, amen."

6. Pray the Binding Prayers

And I will give you the keys of the kingdom of heaven, and whatever you bind on earth will be bound in heaven, and whatever you loose on earth will be loosed in heaven. (Matthew 16:19)

Just as you can bind the devil and his demons, so can you also bind[8] (wrap firmly around) the good things of the Lord to you. Daily bind the following to you and your loved ones. The order is not particularly important.

- I bind my mind to the mind of Christ,
- I bind my will to the will of God,
- I bind my feet to paths of righteousness,

---

8. Strong's #G1210.

- I bind myself to God's Word—the absolute truth,
- I bind myself to the power of the blood of Jesus,
- I bind myself to God's timing, and
- I bind myself to the salvation* accomplished on the cross.

*Salvation[9] includes deliverance, health and healing, protection, peace, and prosperity—literally, wholeness in every area of our lives.

7. Thank Him for His Benefits

Bless the LORD, O my soul;…bless the LORD…and forget not all His benefits….
(Psalm 103:1–2; see also verses 3–5, 20–21)

"I bless You, Lord, for all Your benefits:
- You forgive my sins,
- You heal my diseases,
- You have ransomed me from death,
- You surround me with love and tender mercies,
- You fill my life with good things,
- You renew my youth like the eagle's,
- You see to it that I am treated fairly, and
- You give me angels to carry out the word I speak.
- I marvel at Your great love for me!"

8. Study the Word of God

Open my eyes so that I can see wonderful truths in your law.
(Psalm 119:18 NIrV)

---
9. Strong's #G4991.

Be led by the Holy Spirit; ask the Lord what He wants you to read and study. Use a version of the Bible that is easy for you to understand. Read for revelation knowledge from the Holy Spirit, not quantity.

9. Pray in the Spirit

I will pray with the spirit, and I will also pray with the understanding.... (1 Corinthians 14:15)

Spend quality time every day praying in the Spirit to quiet your mind and to get the mind of God. (See "Prayer for Baptism in the Holy Spirit" on page 260.)

10. Journal

Write down the revelation and make it plain on tablets.... (Habakkuk 2:2 NIV)

Journaling is important in our pursuit of intimacy with God. Record your prayer requests and the answers He provides, as well as the things He reveals to you as you ask Him these questions:

1. "What do You want to say to me today?"
2. "Where do You want me to go today?"
3. "Whom do You want to touch through me today?"

BLESS THE LORD

One of the most powerful ways to enter into the presence of the Lord and grow in intimacy with Him is to bless Him. Another benefit to blessing the Lord is that it infuriates the devil and sends him packing!

Bless the LORD, O my soul; and all that is within me, bless His holy name! (Psalm 103:1)

Because Your lovingkindness is better than life, my lips shall praise You. Thus I will bless You while I live; I will lift up my hands in Your name. (Psalm 63:3–4)

Blessed are You, LORD God of Israel, our Father, forever and ever. Yours, O LORD, is the greatness, the power and the glory, the victory and the majesty; for all that is in heaven and in earth is Yours; Yours is the kingdom, O LORD, and You are exalted as head over all. Both riches and honor come from You, and You reign over all. In Your hand is power and might; in Your hand it is to make great and to give strength to all. Now therefore, our God, we thank You and praise Your glorious name. (1 Chronicles 29:10–13)

For a more in-depth discussion of worship as a means of drawing close to God, see "Worship" on page 276.

NUCLEAR WEAPONS IN A NUTSHELL

I declare and decree today over _____ (names)
that we have the mind of Christ,
that the wisdom of God flows through us,

that the anointing is upon us,
and that everything our hands touch prospers.

Our eyes and ears are blessed; we catch everything the Spirit of God is showing us today. Everywhere our feet tread, we possess; and we have authority over all the work of the enemy.

I declare that the enemy shall not outwit us!

God will beat down our foes from before our faces and smite those who hate us.

We are covered with the blood of Jesus and surrounded with His hedge of protection.

I declare that no weapon formed against us will prosper!

I charge the ministering angels to go before us to accompany, defend, and protect us in all our ways of service and obedience to Him.

I say that He is our Father and our God; in Him do we trust!

I thank You, Lord, for Your faithfulness, mercy, and loving-kindness, which go before us.

We are anointed to do great things for God on a level the world is not familiar with, all for the glory of God!

We will experience preferential treatment today because we have favor with God and man!

We are blessed and highly favored of the Lord!

—© Gail Winter

PART II:
NUCLEAR STRATEGIES TO BLAST THE DEVIL

DECLARE VICTORY OVER THE FLESH

We are no longer slaves to sin. In Romans chapter 6, Paul urges believers to die to sin so that they may live with Christ. He says that when we do this, we are freed from the law and free to walk in grace. The first thing we must do is confess and repent of our sin.

Prayer of Confession and Repentance

Heavenly Father, I confess to You that I am in bondage to _____. Lord, I ask for Your forgiveness. Please cleanse me of all unrighteousness, and renew a right spirit within me. I ask for greater strength to resist every temptation and to live righteously for You. I cover myself with the Lord Jesus Christ, and make no provision for indulging my flesh. I stop thinking about evil cravings, and, with the help of God, I will not gratify its desires. I declare that I am free! I believe I receive strength and freedom now, in the name of Jesus. Amen.

FREEDOM FROM SIN

The following affirmations are based on the truths found in Romans 6. Say them aloud when you need a reminder that you have already been set free from sin and that you do not need to bow to it any longer!

Declarations of Freedom from Slavery to Sin

- I will not take God's kindness for granted by continuing in sin, even though His grace is great toward me. (See Romans 6:1.)
- I am dead to sin and no longer live under its influence. (See Romans 6:2.)
- Just as Christ was brought back from death to life by the glorious power of the Father, so I, too, shall live a new kind of life. (See Romans 6:4.)
- I know that the person I used to be was nailed to the cross with Christ to put an end to sin in my body. I am no longer at sin's beck and call. (See Romans 6:6.)
- I have been freed from sin because my fleshly nature died with Christ. Likewise, because He lives, I will also live with Him. (See Romans 6:7–8.)
- I consider myself dead to sin's power, instead living for God in the power that Christ Jesus gives me. (See Romans 6:11.)
- I do not let sin rule my physical body, nor do I obey the lusts thereof. I never offer any parts of my body to sin's power. (See Romans 6:12.)
- No part of my body will ever be used to do any ungodly thing. Instead, I offer every part of my body to God to do the things that He approves of. (See Romans 6:13.)
- Sin no longer can tell me how to live. After all, I'm not living under that old tyranny any longer. I am living in the freedom of God. (See Romans 6:14.)
- I am God's servant; I wholeheartedly obey His teachings. (See Romans 6:16–17.)

- I am free from sin. I present my body to God as a servant to righteousness, which leads me to live a holy life. (See Romans 6:19.)
- Now that I have been freed from sin, I have become God's slave. This results in a holy life now and will ultimately result in everlasting life, found in Christ Jesus my Lord. (See Romans 6:22–23.)

Meditate on the following Scripture and personalize it. With God's help and perseverance, you can overcome any ungodly stronghold.

> *But clothe yourself with the Lord Jesus Christ (the Messiah), and make no provision for [indulging] the flesh [put a stop to thinking about the evil cravings of your physical nature] to [gratify its] desires (lusts).* (Romans 13:14 AMP)

Prayer of Victory over the Old Nature

You can pray this prayer over yourself or someone else by inserting the appropriate name(s) in the proper places and changing the pronouns accordingly.

Father God, in the name of Jesus Christ, I bind my spirit, soul, and body to the will and purposes of God. I bind myself to the truth of God's Word. I bind myself to an awareness of the power of the blood of Jesus—its redemption, salvation, healing, deliverance, protection, and prosperity.

I bind my mind to the mind of Christ so that I can have the thoughts, purposes, and feelings of His heart in me. I bind my feet to the paths You have ordained for me to walk, Father, that my steps will be strong and steady, for *"the steps of a good man are ordered by the Lord"* (Psalm 37:23).

I bind myself to the work of the cross with all of its mercy, truth, love, power, forgiveness, and death to self. I declare that I will take up my cross and follow You. (See Mark 8:34.)

According to Mark 3:27, I bind the devil, who is *the* strong man, and loose his hold on everything he has ever stolen from me. I rebuke his works and cancel every attack he has planned against me. I demand that he pay back seven times everything he has stolen from me, including my health, peace, joy, jobs, finances, profits, wealth, and relationships. (See Proverbs 6:31.)

Lord, I repent of having wrong attitudes and thoughts. I renounce them now and ask for Your forgiveness, which I receive by faith in Jesus' name. I loose every old, wrong pattern of thinking, attitude, idea, desire, belief, habit, and behavior that may still be at work within me. I tear down, crush, smash, and destroy every stronghold and excuse I have erected to protect any wrong thinking. I bind myself to the attitudes and patterns of Jesus Christ. I bind myself to the overcoming behavior and spiritual desires that line up with the fruit of the Holy Spirit.

Father, I loose every stronghold in my life that is protecting any wrong feelings I have against or toward anyone. Forgive me, as I forgive those who have caused me pain, loss, or grief. I loose and break off any desire for retribution or revenge. In the name of Jesus, I loose the power and the effects of any harsh words or verbal curses spoken about or to me and my loved ones. I loose all strongholds connected with any curses.

I loose all generational bondages and their strongholds from myself and my loved ones. Thank You, Jesus, that You have promised that whatever I bind and loose on earth will be bound and loosed in heaven. (See Matthew 16:19.) Thank You, Father God, for giving me authority over the powers of darkness and for giving me the keys of the kingdom of heaven. Amen.[10]

Prayer for Others with Addictions

Heavenly Father, thank You that there is nothing too hard for You. Thank You that Jesus was manifested that He might destroy the works of the devil. Heavenly Father, I ask You to set _____ free from every bondage and addiction, in the name of Jesus. Lord, put a desire in his/her heart for righteousness. Thank You in advance for answering my prayer. In Jesus' name, amen.

POSITIONED FOR VICTORY!

There are several definitions of the term "lust." Generally speaking, lust can be defined as dwelling upon a sexual thought. A lustful desire is basically something you should not have. According to the Bible, sexual enjoyment is to be shared only in the context of marriage.

Unfortunately, sexual sins such as adultery, fornication, pornography, homosexuality, and pedophilia seem to trip up Christians as often as unbelievers. This ought not to be so!

You must renew your mind through the Word of God if you are ever to be free from the bondage of sexual sins. Willpower

---

10. Adapted from prayer found in Liberty Savard, *Shattering Your Strongholds: Freedom from Your Struggles* (North Brunswick, NJ: Bridge-Logos, 1992).

alone will never achieve this goal. Even binding demons and going through deliverance sessions will not give lasting results *unless* you renew your mind with the Word. You may be free temporarily; but, most assuredly, those temptations will present themselves again. You must replace your old thoughts with God's thoughts in order to keep yourself from acting on the temptations of lust.

Meditating on the following biblical affirmations and making them your confession will empower you to defeat sexual temptation.

Declarations of Victory over Lust

- God, Your will for my life is to abstain from sexual immorality and any lustful passion that might lead to it. Your Word sanctifies me. (See 1 Thessalonians 4:3–7.)

- I will not let sin reign in my body by obeying its lust, but I will use my body as an instrument of righteousness. (See Romans 6:12.) My spiritual service to You, Lord, is to present my mind, body, soul, and spirit as a living sacrifice to You—holy, acceptable, and blameless. (See Romans 12:1.)

- No lustful thought assigned against me shall prosper, for I will take every thought captive to the obedience of Christ. (See Isaiah 54:17; 2 Corinthians 10:5.)

- I have made a covenant agreement with my eyes not to gaze upon a woman/man lustfully (see Job 31:1), for the lamp of my body is my eyes; and since I focus them on what is pure and godly, my whole body is full of light. But if my eyes gaze upon impure things, then my whole body will be full of darkness. (See Matthew 6:22–23.)

- God, You have transformed my nature and placed in me a new mind and a new heart. I have a good and righteous nature like Yours, Lord. (See Ezekiel 36:26; 2 Peter 1:4; 1 Peter 1:22.)

Therefore, I choose not to look at a woman/man lustfully or be flattered by her/his seduction (see Proverbs 7:5, 21), for I choose to guard my heart with all diligence. (See Proverbs 4:23.)

- Mine is the victory that has overcome the world's system of the lust of the flesh, the lust of the eye, and the boastful pride of life. (See 1 John 2:16.) I defeat this evil world and its temptations by trusting Christ to give me the victory. (See 1 John 5:4.)

- Lust is not my master or lord, for I died with Christ to sin; I no longer lust after anything or any person. (See 1 Peter 4:1–2; Romans 6:11–13.) Jesus is my Master and Lord. I believe and am convinced that I have total victory over any spirits of lust or perversion, for all my enemies are under my feet. (See Ephesians 1:21–22.) I choose to put a stop to their influence by wielding the sword of the Spirit—which is the Word of God—by speaking it and obeying it. (See Ephesians 6:17; Revelation 2:16.)

- I will not prostitute my emotions or affections to anything or any person that is not ordained by God. (See Colossians 3:5.) I will not relate to my sisters/brothers in the Lord in a way that would kindle passion within them or me that I cannot righteously fulfill. (See 1 Corinthians 7:1.)

- I no longer value women/men according to their physical attributes and anatomy, but I regard them by the Spirit. I choose to be spiritually minded and not carnally minded. (See 2 Corinthians 5:16–21.)

- I will not be conformed to the world's system of thinking about women/men as sex objects, but I am transformed by the renewing of my mind (see Romans 12:2), for I view an older woman/man as a mother/father and a younger woman/brother as my sister/brother, in all purity. (See 1 Timothy 5:2.)

WALK IN VICTORY

Once you have declared that you are free, you should no longer say you are in bondage; that would be considered being double-minded, and we know that *"a double minded man is unstable in all his ways"* (James 1:8 KJV). You cannot vacillate between two opinions and expect to receive anything from God. You must be firmly convinced that God has set you free from all addictions and sinful behaviors.

Prayer of Victory over the Flesh

Thank You, heavenly Father, that I am no longer in bondage to _____. Thank You that You give me strength to resist every temptation, so that I can live righteously for You. I keep myself covered with the blood of the Lord Jesus Christ, and make no provision for indulging my flesh. I stop thinking about evil cravings, and, with the help of God, I will not gratify the desires of the flesh. I declare that I am free! I believe I receive strength and freedom now, in the name of Jesus. Amen.

If you stumble, simply repent and continue declaring that in Christ Jesus, you are free from all bondage to sin.

Renew Your Mind

In order to live a victorious life, free from addictions and destructive habits, you absolutely must renew your mind with the Word of God! You can have hands laid on you, you can go through deliverance sessions, you can beg God day and night to free you, but the truth is that you cannot find lasting freedom by dint of your own willpower.

Creflo Dollar says, "If you do not change the way you think, you won't change the way you live."[11] Romans 12:2 certainly confirms that statement:

*And do not be conformed to this world, but **be transformed by the renewing of your mind**, that you may prove what is that good and acceptable and perfect will of God.*

The apostle Paul said it clearly: renewing your mind with the Word of God is the only way that you can ever be free from sinful, destructive behavior.

God's Word is powerful; the earth and all creation were formed when God spoke it into existence. (See Genesis 1.) Jesus says in John 15:7, "*If you abide in Me, and **My words abide in you**, you will ask what you desire, and it shall be done for you.*" Notice that it says, "My words abide in you." God's Word must remain in us at all times.

How does the Word of God remain inside of us? The answer is in the daily confession and mediation of God's Word. God told Joshua that in order for him to be successful and prosperous, he must meditate on His law—which is His Word—day and night. (See Joshua 1:8.)

Here are other Scriptures which show us that putting the Word in our hearts will keep us from sin:

Your word I have hidden in my heart, that I might not sin against You!   (Psalm 119:11)

Walk in the Spirit, and you shall not fulfill the lust of the flesh.   (Galatians 5:16)

Throw off your old sinful nature and your former way of life, which is corrupted by lust and deception. Instead, let the Spirit

---

11. Dollar, *How to Change Your Thinking.*

renew your thoughts and attitudes. Put on your new nature, created to be like God—truly righteous and holy.

(Ephesians 4:22–24 NLT)

Though we walk in the flesh, we do not war according to the flesh. For the weapons of our warfare are not carnal [not of this world] but mighty in God for pulling down strongholds, casting down arguments and every high thing that exalts itself against the knowledge of God, bringing every thought into captivity to the obedience of Christ. (2 Corinthians 10:3–5)

When we begin to confess and meditate upon God's Word, the Word of God will then be hidden inside of us, and we will then begin to do and act according to God's Word. Slowly but surely, we will begin to be transformed by the Word of God.

Nothing pleases God more than to hear His children confessing the Word of God as an expression of their faith in Him.

Follow these steps to renew your mind:

1. *Fellowship* with the Father every day!
2. *Find* specific Scriptures that pertain to your struggles.
3. *Speak* those Scriptures aloud several times a day.
4. *Replace* worldly, sinful thoughts with Word-based thoughts. You must feed your faith and starve your fleshly desires.
5. *Change* your actions! You must *"resist the devil"*; no one can do it for you! But you cannot do this with willpower alone. You must use the weapons that He provides—His Word, His name, His blood, His armor—and also ask for the help of the Holy Spirit.

6. *Study* your Bible and believe what it says. If you do not read your Bible, you will not know if what you are thinking and doing lines up with the Word of God.

7. *Separate* yourself from all ungodly situations and from the people who might try to influence you to get back into the old patterns of behavior.

It is not easy, but you must study, meditate on, and speak the Word of God every day. As His Word gets down into your heart, your thinking and behavior will begin to change. Do not get discouraged if you do not see immediate results. Continue to exercise faith and patience until your freedom is manifested.

To obtain victory over lust, it would help you tremendously to be baptized in the Holy Spirit with the evidence of speaking in tongues. Praying in your prayer language every day will give you the strength you need to resist temptations. (See "Baptism in the Holy Spirit" on page 259.)

Spend quality time in the Bible, meditating on and memorizing applicable verses. Hiding God's Word in your heart will stop any mental temptations. The psalmist both prayed *and* hid God's Word in his heart so that he would not sin against God: *"Do not let me stray from your commands. I have hidden your word in my heart that I might not sin against you"* (Psalm 119:10–11 NIV). If you truly desire lasting deliverance, you must follow this example.

In summary, victory over sin is found not just in what you do but also in what you do not do. For example, you must stop thinking about how good it would feel to gratify those sinful desires. Rather, you must starve the old, sinful nature, instead feeding your spirit with God's Word by meditating on the Scriptures and speaking the Word of God out loud. Your voluntary thoughts—that is, the thoughts you *choose* to ponder—are extremely important.

Keep in mind Romans 8:5, which says, *"Those who live according to the sinful nature have their minds set on what that nature desires; but those who live in accordance with the Spirit have their minds set on what the Spirit desires."*

Agree with God's Word

Consider this: One weapon that satan will use to try to stop you from changing your behavior is discouragement. He wants you to think you cannot change—that it is impossible for you to let go of old habits. Do not believe him for a minute! Put your confidence in God and His Word. Believe what He has said about you, and know that when the Word is on the inside of you, you will be equipped to make decisions that keep you on the path to change. Remember, as Mike Murdock has said, no one has been a loser longer than satan.

KNOW YOUR IDENTITY IN CHRIST JESUS

Satan is a liar and the father of all lies. (See John 8:44.) He is the accuser of the brethren, and accuses us before the throne of God. (See Revelation 12:10.) If we do not know who we are *in Christ*, then we will easily believe the lies of the devil. When he tells us that we are worthless, that we have done too many horrible things for God to use us, we will believe him.

I am what God says I am, regardless of how I feel about myself, or even how others feel about me. My feelings cannot change the absolute truth of God's Word. God's opinion of me matters more than anyone else's!

We need to learn who we are *in Christ* and affirm it out loud every day! When the devil comes to you and says, "Who do you think you are?" you can tell him exactly who you are *in Christ*!

Confession of Who I Am, According to God

My heavenly Father says...

- I am Christ's ambassador. (See 2 Corinthians 5:20.)
- I have been sent into the world. (See John 17:18.)
- I am a fisher of men. (See Matthew 4:19.)
- I am the salt of the earth. (See Matthew 5:13.)
- I am the light of the world. (See Matthew 5:14.)

- When I ask for something in faith, according to the will of God, I will receive it. (See Mark 11:23–24.)
- When I ask, I'll receive; when I seek, I'll find; when I knock, the door will be opened to me. (See Luke 11:9–10.)
- I have passed from death into life. (See John 5:24.)
- I now have eternal life. (See John 3:36.)
- The Holy Spirit is flowing out of my inner being. (See John 7:38.)
- The truth has set me free (including free of wrong thinking). (See John 8:32.)
- If I ask anything in Jesus' name that God has promised, He will do it. (See John 14:14.)
- I am loved by Jesus. (See John 15:9.)
- I am protected from the evil one. (See John 17:15.)
- I am sanctified by the truth of God's Word. (See John 17:17.)
- I have God's glory and anointing. (See John 17:22.)
- Christ is in me, and I am loved by the Father. (See John 17:23.)
- I have forgiveness of sins *through Christ*. (See Acts 13:38.)
- I have been freed from all bondages. (See Acts 13:39.)
- I am the righteousness of God *in Christ Jesus*! (See 2 Corinthians 5:21.)

WHO I AM IN CHRIST JESUS

The moment you made Jesus your Lord, you were re-created by God. The old man—your unregenerate spirit man—was replaced by a new man, created in Christ Jesus. You were born of the Spirit of God. A seed was sown in your heart—the incorruptible seed of God's Word—and you were placed *in Christ Jesus*.

Scriptures that refer to being *"in Christ," "in Him," "by whom,"* and so on, occur 134 times in the Bible. Find those Scriptures and study them carefully. Whatever the Word says about you belongs to you because now you are *in Christ Jesus*!

Below are some examples of your true identity *in Him*. You may not feel like the statements are true at all about you. However, the more you reaffirm who you are *in Christ*, the more your behavior will come into alignment with who God says you are. You simply have to believe and receive it by faith.

Confession of Who I Am in Christ

In Christ…

- I am a child of God. (See Romans 8:16.)
- I am deeply loved by my Father. (See 1 John 3:1.)
- I am a joint-heir with Christ. (See Romans 8:17.)
- I am God's special handiwork. (See Ephesians 2:10.)
- I have obtained salvation with eternal glory. (See 2 Timothy 2:10.)
- I am a new creation. (See 2 Corinthians 5:17.)
- I no longer live, but Christ lives in me. (See Galatians 2:20.)
- I am in right standing with God. (See 2 Corinthians 5:21.)
- I have been delivered from the power of darkness. (See Colossians 1:13.)
- I have been translated into the kingdom of God. (See Colossians 1:13.)
- I now sit in heavenly places. (See Ephesians 2:6.)

- I have redemption through Jesus' blood. (See Colossians 1:14.)
- I have forgiveness of sins. (See Colossians 1:14.)
- I have no condemnation. (See Romans 8:1.)
- I am holy and without blame. (See Ephesians 1:4.)
- I am more than a conqueror. (See Romans 8:37.)
- I always triumph. (See 2 Corinthians 2:14.)
- I can quench all the fiery darts of the wicked one. (See Ephesians 6:16.)
- I have overcome the devil, the flesh, and the world. (See 1 John 4:4.)
- I am accepted by God. (See Ephesians 1:6.)
- I am anointed to do great things for God. (See 1 John 2:27.)
- I am a sweet fragrance to God. (See 2 Corinthians 2:15.)
- I have abundant mercy from God. (See 1 Peter 1:3.)
- Nothing can separate me from the love of God. (See Romans 8:38–39.)
- I am redeemed from the curse of the law. (See Galatians 3:13.)
- I have the blessings of Abraham. (See Galatians 3:14.)
- I am blessed with all spiritual blessings in heavenly places. (See Ephesians 1:3.)
- I have the exceeding riches of God's grace and kindness. (See Ephesians 2:7.)
- I have God's strength and ability. (See Philippians 4:13.)
- I am a work in progress. (See Philippians 1:6.)
- My mind is renewed and enlightened. (See 2 Corinthians 3:14.)
- I have the peace of God which passes all understanding. (See Philippians 4:7.)

- I can do all things. (See Philippians 4:13.)
- All of my needs are met. (See Philippians 4:19.)
- I am born of God, and the evil one cannot touch me. (See 1 John 5:18–19.)
- I have abundant love. (See 1 Timothy 1:14.)
- I have an ever-living hope. (See 1 Peter 1:3.)
- I have joy unspeakable. (See 1 Peter 1:8.)
- I am established and grounded in the Word. (See 1 Peter 5:10.)
- I have fellowship with all believers. (See 1 John 1:7.)
- God lives in me. (See 1 John 4:15.)
- I have been given the Spirit of God. (See 1 John 3:24.)
- I am led by the Spirit of God. (See Romans 8:14.)
- I have received the anointing which teaches me all things. (See 1 John 2:27.)
- I have received the spirit of wisdom and revelation knowledge. (See Ephesians 1:17.)

YOU ARE ANOINTED!

Did you know that if you have been born again and are abiding *in Christ*, you have the same anointing as Jesus? The Bible says, *"The anointing which you have received from Him abides in you"* (1 John 2:27). The anointing is a special endowment given by the Holy Spirit to anyone who will receive it. This anointing produces miraculous power and the ability to do extraordinary things.

You were created in the image of God not just to be normal! There is a special anointing that God has put on the inside of you to do outstanding, incredible things for the kingdom of God, all for the glory of God!

But the anointing is not automatic. You must speak it out loud every day for it to be powerful and effective. Remember, by your words, you call into existence the things you desire. (See Romans 4:17.) Below are some examples of declarations to make daily. You may want to compose your own statements, as well, to fit your needs and desires.

Bold Declarations of Anointing[12]

- *I am anointed* to do great things for God on a level the world is not familiar with, all for the glory of God!
- *I am anointed* to win souls on a level the world is not familiar with, all for the glory of God!
- *I am anointed* to pray and praise on a level the world is not familiar with, all for the glory of God!
- *I am anointed* to walk in love on a level the world is not familiar with, all for the glory of God!
- *I am anointed* to lay hands on the sick and see them recover speedily, on a level the world is not familiar with, all for the glory of God!
- *I am anointed* for my job/business/ministry on a level the world is not familiar with, all for the glory of God!
- *I am anointed* to walk in divine health—to stay healthy and fit—on a level the world is not familiar with, all for the glory of God!
- *Our marriage is anointed* on a level the world is not familiar with, all for the glory of God!

---

12. Inspired by Chip Brim, *Life's Victories through the Anointing* (audio teaching).

EXERCISE YOUR AUTHORITY

"Be aggressive. Start saying 'no' to the devil! Stop entertaining the thoughts he throws your way. Instead, speak the Word right in his face!"
—Jerry Savelle

As far as the believer is concerned, the devil is already defeated. He and his demons were whipped when Jesus *"disarmed principalities and powers, He made a public spectacle of them, **triumphing over them by the cross**"* (Colossians 2:15). First Corinthians 15:57 (AMP) says, *"But thanks be to God, who gives us the victory [making us conquerors] through our Lord Jesus Christ."* And Ephesians 1:19–23 states that Jesus Christ defeated satan when He rose from the dead, and now He is sitting at the right hand of the Father, far above all the principalities and powers of evil. Our victory is a continuation of the victory Christ secured when He bruised the head of the serpent at Calvary. (See Romans 16:20.)

So, where is satan's place now? Satan's place is under our feet! He has no more legal right to us. He may "strike our heel" and aggravate us (see Genesis 3:15), but we can crush his head because Christ Jesus defeated him. We have been empowered by God Almighty with mighty weapons to stand up to the devil when he comes against us!

Often, we act as though we are helpless against the trials, tribulations, and temptations satan puts in our path. Yet God has made available to us everything we need to overcome our adversary.

VICTORY IS UP TO YOU

Satan has been defeated, but he hasn't yet been destroyed. You must take authority over him every day of your life until Jesus return to the earth to set up His kingdom. Only then will satan be forever bound and unable to afflict us anymore. In the meantime, you must take authority over him and let him know he cannot harass you and your loved ones. Satan does not care if you have authority over him, as long as you do not exercise it.[13]

Again, satan has no power in the life of a believer—except what we allow! As long as we abide *in Christ Jesus*, the devil cannot harm us. (See Psalm 91.) This section will help you to understand who you are *in Christ*, and will teach you how to exercise your authority as a believer, so that you keep the devil under your feet.

THE WEAPONS OF YOUR WARFARE

Let's start at the beginning. In Genesis 1:26, God gave Adam dominion (authority) over the whole earth. Adam was in charge, until Eve was deceived by the serpent and they both disobeyed God. At that time, Adam lost his authority, and satan assumed dominion over him—and all mankind.

But the story doesn't end there! God had a plan that would deliver a death blow to satan and reinstate mankind's authority. This is what Christ's crucifixion and resurrection accomplished for

---

13. Dr. Larry Ollison, "The Cutting Edge" Devotional. Online. http://www.larryollison.com/cuttingedge/the-cutting-edge-devotional.

> "TRAGEDY IS NOT A SIGN OF GOD'S SOVEREIGNTY BUT A SIGN OF THE DEVIL'S WORKS. USE YOUR AUTHORITY TO STOP HIM!"
> —TOM BROWN

us. He won back our authority when He "*disarmed principalities and powers*" (Colossians 2:15) He triumphed over the devil—and He did it for you!

"Wait!" you might say. "If satan is defeated, then why do *I* always feel defeated? Why does it seem like he is always 'eating my lunch'? Why have things never worked out for me?"

Again, you are walking around defeated and beat up because you do not realize that it is your responsibility to resist the devil! You are the one with dominion now. You must put satan under your feet. Jesus already did His part; it is now your responsibility to *enforce* satan's defeat.

When we resist the devil, we are reminding him that Jesus won the battle, that he is defeated, and that he has no authority over the church. The most effective way we can do this is to use the Word of God against him. When satan hears you speak the Word of God, he knows then that you know your rights, and he must stop his attack. But, remember—the devil will take full advantage of you until you exercise your authority.

Even after "reading him his rights," you will have to continue to resist the devil and his cohorts. For the rest of your life, it will be necessary for you to be intensely proactive. Continually put him in his place by speaking the Word of God, claiming the name of Jesus, and applying the blood of Jesus. You absolutely must visualize you and your loved ones as radioactive to the devil, and you must remind him of that every day!

Let me explain it another way. In Luke 19, Jesus told a parable and said, "[A certain nobleman] *called his ten servants, and delivered them ten pounds, and said unto them, Occupy till I come*" (Luke 19:13 KJV). The word *occupy* is a military term. You have heard of military "occupying forces," haven't you? This is what we are: *occupying forces!*

An occupying force is sent in only *after* the war is won. The force simply occupies the territories by stopping any pockets of resistance that may still be lurking in the region.

In fact, the devil's battle against us looks very much like guerrilla warfare, in which rebels refuse to acknowledge the right of the legitimate government to rule. Plain and simple, we are the legitimate rulers. But satan and his cohorts are the rebels trying to rob us of our kingdom rights as believers.

Everything we want in life—health and healing, protection, provision, and so on—has to be fought for every day!

And Jesus gives us the authority to fight for these things. He does not leave anyone unprepared. In Luke chapter 10, Jesus gave authority to the seventy disciples before He sent them out:

> *Behold! I have given you authority and power to trample upon serpents and scorpions, and [physical and mental strength and ability] over all the power that the enemy [possesses]; and nothing shall in any way harm you.* (Luke 10:19 AMP)

Then, we read that Jesus gave the same authority to *everyone* who believes in Him:

> *These signs will accompany those who believe: in my name they will cast out demons; they will speak in new tongues; they will pick up serpents with their hands; and if they drink any deadly poison, it will not hurt them; they will lay their hands on the sick, and they will recover.* (Mark 16:17–18)

DECLARE YOUR AUTHORITY OVER THE ENEMY

You must exercise your authority *on purpose*! How? Daily you must keep the devil in his place with bold declarations and prayers, such as the following.

Declarations of Authority over the Devil

- Devil, I come with the authority that was given to me to carry out the Great Commission by the power of the blood of the Lamb! Take your hands off _____ (name the situation/person), and stop this attack now!

- Satan, I stand on the authority of God's Word in Psalm 89:22–24 (AMP):

[God says,] *"The enemy shall not exact from him or do him violence or outwit him, nor shall the wicked afflict and humble him. I will beat down his foes before his face and smite those who hate him. My faithfulness and My mercy and lovingkindness shall be with him, and in My name shall his horn be exalted [great power and prosperity shall be conferred upon him]."*

- I declare that you will not outwit us; you will not trick us or steal from us, nor will you try to make us pay a debt that Jesus has already paid! God Himself will beat down our foes from before our faces and smite those who hate us. Devil, I'm giving you fair warning—we are God's property, so take your hands off of us, in Jesus' name! God's faithfulness and mercy and lovingkindness go before us, and in His name great power and prosperity are conferred upon us. I say, "He is our Father, our God, and the Rock of our Salvation."

- Father, I declare that I am a believer. I use my authority in the name of Jesus and force the enemy out of my life!

- The following signs accompany me: In Jesus' name, I drive out demons; I speak in new languages (tongues); I pick up serpents (that is, I can deal with demonic powers); and even if I drink anything deadly, it will not hurt me. I lay my hands on the sick, and they recover. (See Mark 16:17–18 AMP.) Greater is He that is in me than he that is in the world. (See 1 John 4:4.) I submit myself to God; I resist the devil, and he must flee. (See James 4:7.) Thank You, Father, for the authority You have given to me. In Jesus' name, amen.

Declarations of a Hedge of Protection

- Father God, I thank You that the blood of Jesus is the hedge against the destroyer. You surround all our households and everything we have with Your hedge of protection, and Your wall of fire is around about us. (See Zechariah 2:5.) The Lord has granted us long life and has preserved us from destruction. (See Job 10:12.)

- Today I declare Your complete protection over us against accident, incident, injury, disease, and illness, and from sexual, emotional, spiritual, physical, and financial damage. I declare Your hedge of protection, Lord. Thank You for protection from the wiles of the evil one and from every demonic power.

- I declare that no matter what happens around us, we have a covenant of peace (that is, wholeness and security) with God. His love, kindness, and protection will never depart from us. (See Isaiah 54:10.)

- Because we dwell in the Secret Place of the Most High God, we abide under the shadow of the Almighty. The Lord is our

Refuge and Fortress. He delivers us from the enemy; therefore, we do not fear the terror in the night or the destruction that takes place at noonday. When we call on the Lord, He immediately answers us. He is with us in trouble; He always delivers us. (See Psalm 91:1–6, 10–11, 15–16.)

- We are the redeemed of the Lord and are in covenant with Jehovah God; therefore, sickness and disease, poverty and lack, fear and oppression have no power over us. We walk in divine health and are physically fit. Our souls prosper because we meditate in God's Word day and night. (See Psalm 1:2.)

- We fear no evil, because the Holy Spirit comforts us. (See Psalm 23:4.) He lives inside of us. God has hedged us in with His protection, and nothing can touch us there. (See Job 1:10.) Greater is He who is in us than he who is in the world! (See 1 John 4:4.)

AUTHORITY TO BIND

If you are born again, you absolutely, positively have authority over satan and his evil demons. Luke 10:19 says, *"Behold, I give you the authority to trample on serpents and scorpions, and over all the power of the enemy, and nothing shall by any means hurt you."*

God intends for the body of Christ to put the devil in his rightful place—under our feet! Keep your foot on that scoundrel's neck at all times, as Jesse Duplantis says. Keep the pressure on him to stop his illegal assault against you and your loved ones.

When Jesus was raised from the dead, He stripped satan of his authority over mankind. That authority has been delegated to the body of Christ in the earth. We are to exercise our authority against satan, thereby destroying his plans, schemes, and evil plots.

You annihilate satan's evil plan by issuing a spoken command to him that he is bound and must leave!

Jesus said, *"I will give you the keys of the kingdom of heaven"* (Matthew 16:19). Then, He tells us what those keys are—the keys of binding and loosing. He says, *"Whatever you bind on earth will be bound in heaven, and whatever you loose on earth will be loosed in heaven."*

> "SATAN DOESN'T CARE IF YOU HAVE AUTHORITY, AS LONG AS YOU DON'T USE IT."
> —DR. LARRY OLLISON

Jesus referred to binding and loosing as the keys of the kingdom, which means that they must be very important. Binding is like a temporary spiritual handcuffing. You can bind a demon spirit, much like tying something up with rope or chains. You cannot bind a person's free will, but you can bind the demons affecting or influencing that person.

What does it mean to bind on earth? It refers to your physical location—right here and now, while you are here on earth. Jesus is saying that the authority to bind and loose is provided for us to use while here on earth.

What does it mean for something to be bound in heaven? If you look up the word "heaven" in the Greek, you'll find another word called "air," which is where the spirits dwell. This isn't referring to heaven as in the place we go after we die, but rather a realm in the atmosphere. So, the word *"heaven"* here is referring to the spiritual realm—the air, where the spirits dwell and operate. In Ephesians 2:2, satan is known as the *"prince of the power of the air."*

So then, when you bind something here on earth, it will be bound in the spiritual realm, as well. This gives us the ability to bind demons, because they dwell within the spiritual realm.

First Things First

Matthew 12:29 tells us the first step we must take to stop the enemy's attack: "*How can one enter a strong man's house and plunder his goods, **unless he first binds the strong man?** And then he will plunder his house.*" You could think of it like this: satan has stolen your "goods"—your health, wealth, and relationships—and taken them to his house. Now, you want to get them back; but he is quite powerful, so first you must overpower him and bind him—handcuff and tie him up, so to speak. Then and only then can you go barging in and get your stuff!

The devil is *the* primary strong man—the commander-in-chief of darkness, so to speak—so, he is the first one you must bind. Speak directly to satan as you enforce your authority as a believer. Once he is bound, then you can go into his "house"—his spiritual kingdom and domain—and force him to give back what he has stolen from you. It may be health, finances, relationships, hindering your children from being saved, and so on.

Breaking Spiritual Strongholds

Satan has a hierarchy in the kingdom of darkness, as described in Ephesians 6:12. We learn from this Scripture and others that not every demon is a strong man. There are "head" demons, which rule over a particular group of smaller ones. These "head" demons act as the "strong man" over a particular demon or group of demons that are causing issues in any one person or circumstance.

In Jerry and Carol Robeson's book *Strongman's His Name… What's His Game?* they offer excellent insights on effective spiritual warfare.[14] Instead of binding *symptoms*, we can attack the sixteen strong men, or demonic spirits, mentioned by name in the Bible. Once their powers are broken, the demons are helpless.

For help in classifying the sixteen strongmen, refer to the chart on pages 78–82, which lists them with the symptoms they produce. Locate the symptoms that a person is exhibiting, and then identify the strong man. Many times, there are two or more strong men working together, so ask the Holy Spirit to reveal all of them to you.

The "Nuclear Bomb" of Binding

In the name of Jesus…

- I bind my mind to the mind of Christ.
- I bind my will and desires to God's will and purposes for my life.
- I bind myself to the truth of God and the love of God.
- I bind my finances to God's unlimited resources.
- I bind my future to God's infinite wisdom and design for my life.
- I bind my body to the resurrection life of Jesus.
- I bind my spirit, soul, and body to the blood of Jesus.
- I bind myself to the Word of God, which will *renew my mind* and *set me free*.
- And, Father, I bind my heart to Your heart.

---

14. See Jerry and Carol Robeson, *Strongman's His Name…What's His Game?* (New Kensington, PA: Whitaker House, 1984.)

AUTHORITY TO LOOSE

In Luke 13:11–16, Jesus healed a woman who had been bound eighteen years by a spirit of infirmity. He said to her, *"Woman, you are loosed from your infirmity"* (Luke 13:12), thereby casting out the spirit. When the synagogue ruler objected to Him healing on the Sabbath, Jesus replied, *"Ought not this woman, being a daughter of Abraham, whom Satan has bound—think of it—for eighteen years, be loosed from this bond on the Sabbath?"* (Luke 13:16)

This story in is important in that it demonstrates that we can loose sickness. The Greek word for *"loosed"* here is *apoluo*, meaning "let go...put (send) away, release, set at liberty."[15]

In John 11:39–44, Lazarus was still bound after he was given new life. He had grave clothes still wrapped around him. Jesus told His disciples, *"Loose him, and let him go"* (John 11:44). It is up to us to loose the "grave clothes" of sickness and disease (cancer, diabetes, heart disease, etc.). We are to loose our bodies—and those of our loved ones—from the evil powers that cause sickness, sorrow, unsoundness, unhappiness, torment, captivity, and so forth.

The other side of the coin, so to speak, is to loose—to release or allow—the Holy Spirit and the angels to do God's will. We can loose (allow, invite) the good things God has for us that will strengthen our faith and establish our victory.

Declarations of Loosing

The following are examples of loosing.

In the name of Jesus...

- I loose myself/_____ (name) from sickness and infirmity.
- I loose myself from the works of satan, his demons, and his influence in this situation.

---

15. Strong's #G630.

- I loose myself from doubt and unbelief, and all preconceived ideas about healing.
- I loose myself from spiritual blindness.
- I loose myself from any confusion that is going on in my life and body.
- I loose myself from the negative influences of the world.
- I loose myself from all wrong attitudes and patterns of thinking and wrong belief systems.

When praying for others, insert their names as you pray. Instead of imposing our will and desires upon others, we allow and invite God's intervention in a given situation, according to His wisdom and perfect will for each person. Speak the Scripture-based declarations out loud often. As you do, sense knowledge (that is, what you see with you natural senses) just gives way—surrenders—as your mind conforms to the truth of God's Word.

The "Nuclear Bomb" of Loosing

In the name of Jesus...

- I loose and break off from my life any devices of the enemy intended to hinder, deceive, kill, steal, or destroy.
- I loose the power and effects of any damaging words spoken about me, to me, or by me.
- I loose and break off from my life every wrong agreement I've ever entered into, whether with persons, spirits, or ideas.
- I loose and break off from me every wrong belief that I've ever had about God and His will for me, and His will for others.

I loose and break off any bondage hidden within my soul. (Be specific: addictions, bad habits, anger, fear, physical illness, strife, etc.)

DON'T BIND THE SYMPTOMS—BIND THE STRONG MAN!

BIND	SYMPTOMS	LOOSE
Spirit of Divination Acts 16:16–18	Rebellion, Drugs, Magic, Fortuneteller-Soothsayer, Warlock/Witch, Sorcerer, Stargazer/Zodiac, Horoscopes, Hypnotist-Enchanter, Water/Witching, Divination	*Holy Spirit and Gifts* 1 Corinthians 12:9–12
Perverse Spirit Isaiah 19:14	Pornography, Child Abuse, Incest, Sex Perversions, Filthy Mind, Abortion, Evil Actions, Chronic Worrier, Foolish, Atheist, Twisting the Word, Doctrinal Error, Broken Spirit	*God's Spirit; Pureness, Holiness* Zechariah 12:10; Hebrews 10:29
Spirit of Infirmity Luke 13:11–13	Cancer, Asthma/Hay Fever/Allergies, Arthritis, Heart Trouble, Lingering Disorders, Weakness, Bent Body/Spine, Impotent/Frail/Lame, Oppression, Inability to regain strength once a disease sets in, i.e. MS, Hypertension, Diabetes, Parkinson's, MD, Glaucoma, etc.	*Spirit of Life & Gifts of Healing, Praise* Romans 8:2; 1 Corinthians 12:9

Part II: Nuclear Strategies to Blast the Devil

DON'T BIND THE SYMPTOMS—BIND THE STRONG MAN!		
BIND	**SYMPTOMS**	**LOOSE**
Seducing Spirit 1 Timothy 4:1	Hypocritical Lies, Deception, Seared Conscience, Fascination to Evil Ways, Attractions/Fascination with False Prophets, Signs and Wonders, Seducers/Enticers, Wander from Truth	*Holy Spirit and Truth* John 16:13
Familiar Spirit Leviticus 19:31	Medium, Yoga, Clairvoyant, Necromancer, False Prophecy, Passive Mind/Dreamers, Peeping and Muttering, Spiritist	*Holy Spirit and Gifts* 1 Corinthians 12:9–12
Spirit of Haughtiness (Pride) Proverbs 16:18	Prideful, Arrogant/Smug, Obstinate, Self-Righteous, Scornful, Rebellious, Idleness, Strife, Contentious, Rejection of God, Self-Deception	*Humble and Contrite Spirit* Proverbs 16:19; Romans 1:4
Dumb and Deaf Spirit Mark 9:17–29	Dumb-Mute, Crying, Mental Illness, Ear Problems, Blindness, Seizures/Epilepsy, Tearing, Foaming at Mouth, Gnashing Teeth, Pining Away, Prostration, Suicidal	*Resurrection Life and Gifts of Healing* Romans 8:11; 1 Corinthians 12:9

DON'T BIND THE SYMPTOMS—BIND THE STRONG MAN!		
BIND	SYMPTOMS	LOOSE
Spirit of Antichrist 1 John 4:3	Denies Deity of Christ, Humanism, Denies Atonement, Teachers of Heresies, Deceiver, Against Christ and His Teaching, Worldly Speech and Actions, Anti-Christian, Lawlessness	*Spirit of Truth* 1 John 4:6
Spirit of Jealousy Numbers 5:14	Murder, Anger/Rage, Strife, Revenge/Spite, Jealousy, Hatred, Envy, Contention, Cruelty, Extreme Competition, Cause Divisions	*Love of God* 1 Corinthians 13; Ephesians 5:2
Spirit of Heaviness Isaiah 61:3	Excessive Mourning, Sorrow Grief, Broken Heart, Insomnia, Depression, Self-pity, Inner Hurts/Torn Spirit, Despair/Dejection/Hopelessness, Heaviness, Suicidal Thoughts	*Joy, Comforter, Spirit of Praise* John 15:26; Isaiah 61:3
Spirit of Bondage Romans 8:15	Fears, Addictions (drugs, alcohol, tobacco, foods, etc.), Fear of Death, Compulsive Sin, Captivity to Satan, Bondage to Sin, Servant of Corruption	*Liberty, Spirit of Adoption* Romans 8:15

Part II: Nuclear Strategies to Blast the Devil 81

DON'T BIND THE SYMPTOMS—BIND THE STRONG MAN!		
BIND	**SYMPTOMS**	**LOOSE**
Spirit of Error 1 John 4:6	New Age Movement, Error, Servant of Corruption, Unsubmissive. Defensive/ Argumentative, Contentions	*Spirit of Truth* 1 John 4:6; Psalm 51:10
Lying Spirit 2 Chronicles 18:22	Accusations, Gossip, Lies, Flattery, Superstitions, False Teachers, False Prophecy, Strong Deception, Religious Bondages	*Spirit of Truth (Jesus)* John 14:17; 15:26; 16:13
Spirit of Whoredoms Hosea 5:4	Unfaithfulness/ Adultery, Fornication, Prostitution, Idolatry (Spirit, Soul, or Body), Love of Money, Excessive Appetite, Worldliness, Chronic Dissatisfaction	*Spirit of God; Pure Spirit* Ephesians 3:16
Spirit of Fear 2 Timothy 1:7	Fears/Phobias (Claustrophobia, etc.), Fear of Death, Anxiety Attacks/Stress, Heart Attacks, Nightmares/ Terrors, Fear of Man, Untrusting, Doubt, Torment, Horror	*Joy, Love, Power, and a Sound Mind* 2 Timothy 1:7

DON'T BIND THE SYMPTOMS—BIND THE STRONG MAN!		
BIND	SYMPTOMS	LOOSE
Spirit of Death Not mentioned specifically by name	Extreme Oppression, "dark cloud" hanging over, Premature Death (Death is more than just a condition or term; in 1 Corinthians 15:26, Paul says that death is *"the last enemy."*)	*Spirit of Life* Proverbs 10:2
It is always appropriate to loose the fruit of the Spirit: love, joy, peace, longsuffering, kindness, goodness, faithfulness, gentleness, and self-control.		

Lasting Results

Once you have identified and bound the strong man/strong men, command him/them not to return. "[Jesus] *rebuked the unclean spirit, saying to it, 'Deaf and dumb spirit, I command you, come out of him and enter him no more!'"* (Mark 9:25). Then, loose the angelic forces of almighty God to carry through with the deliverance. Angels are *"ministering spirits sent forth to minister for those who will inherit salvation"* (Hebrews 1:14). They are messengers who work on our behalf.

Next, you should loose the strong man's hold upon your stolen possessions—whether spiritual or natural.

After that, you should loose the opposite spirit(s), and the fruit of the Spirit to fill the vacancy. For example, bind hate, loose love; bind pride, loose humility; and so on. Where satan has been commanded to leave, fill the void with God's presence and the fruit of His Spirit, based on Matthew 12:43–45:

*When an unclean spirit goes out of a man, he goes through dry places, seeking rest, and finds none. Then he says, "I will return to my house from which I came." And **when he comes, he finds it empty**, swept, and put in order. Then he goes and takes with him seven other spirits more wicked than himself, and they enter and dwell there; and the last state of that man is worse than the first. So shall it also be with this wicked generation.* (Matthew 12:43–45)

Here are some steps to assist you in breaking spiritual strongholds:

STEP 1: First, bind *the* strong man. You can say something like this: "Satan, according to the authority vested in me in Matthew 18:18, I bind you and render you helpless in _____/this situation. As a matter of record, you are hereby bound, in the name of Jesus."

STEP 2: Next, bind the strong man you have previously identified, and command it not to return. You could say: "I bind you, spirit of _____. You are the strong man trying to exalt yourself over _____'s life. I remind you that your strong man, the devil, has been bound; therefore, you are powerless. Stop and desist your activity in _____ now, in Jesus' name! I command you to never return, according to Mark 9:25."

STEP 3: Next, loose the ministering spirits. You can say: "Ministering spirits, I loose you, in the name of Jesus, to minister on _____'s behalf in this situation, according to the will of God."

STEP 4: Then, release the opposite spirit as per the chart, and also the fruit of the Spirit. You can say: "Father God, I release a spirit of _____, and the fruit of the Holy Spirit. Fill _____ to overflowing with Your presence and power."

STEP 5: Finally, thank God. Say, "Thank You, Father God, that satan is bound and no longer able to work in this situation.

Thank You for giving me the keys of the kingdom of heaven. In Jesus' name, amen."

The ultimate choice is yours whether or not to receive freedom from God. Jesus asked the man at the pool of Bethesda, *"Wilt thou be made whole?"* (John 5:6 KJV). His attitude is still the same: "Do you want to stay the way you are, or do you want to be made whole?" The choice is yours. God has already provided the way out for you.

Bind, Then Remind!

Do not give the faith command again. Persistently remind satan that you've broken his power, and he has no choice but to go. At first, he might test you to see how serious you are. Do not let him fool you; continue to believe and speak the desired answer. Keep thanking God out loud that His power is working on your behalf.

Do not wait for a physical confirmation to prove that something has happened. It may appear as if nothing has changed; however, a great spiritual process was set in motion the moment you uttered God's Word in faith. The victory is always ours if we believe and do not give up.

When Jesus cursed the fig tree, the roots died immediately, but there was no visible proof of that reality right away, because the roots are below the surface and cannot be seen. It took time for the results to be seen—it was not until the following day that the disciples saw that the fig tree had died. (See Mark 11:20–21.) In the same way, it may also take time for the answer to your prayers to be manifested.

It was because of her persistence that the widow in the parable of the unjust judge won her suit. (See Luke 18:1–8.) We are to be equally persistent; to say to God, like the widow pleaded the judge, *"Avenge me of mine adversary"* (Luke 18:3 KJV).

We know that He will honor our plea, for He is our avenger.

And will not [our just] God defend and protect and avenge His elect (His chosen ones), who cry to Him day and night? Will He defer them and delay help on their behalf? I tell you, **He will defend and protect and avenge them speedily.**
(Luke 18:7–8 AMP)

An uproar from the city! A voice from the temple! The voice of the Lord, rendering recompense to His enemies!
(Isaiah 66:6 AMP)

If he is found out, he must restore seven times [what he stole]; he must give the whole substance of his house [if necessary—to meet his fine]. (Proverbs 6:31 AMP)

Let's close this discussion of binding and loosing with a prayer to our great Avenger:

Prayer of Binding and Loosing

Heavenly Father, like the widow woman in Luke 18, I've had enough! I'm asking for justice, and You, God, are the Righteous Judge of all the earth. So, Father, *avenge me of my adversary speedily!* Stop this harassment; cause the attacks to cease, in Jesus' name.

Father, according to Isaiah 66:6, You are the God of recompense. Because satan has been found to be the thief, he is required to compensate me for the damages he has caused. Father, force him to compensate me for everything he has stolen from me. I am asking for no less than seven times restoration, as You provided for me in Proverbs 6:31. Thank You in advance, Lord, for forcing him to pay up!

Thank You, Father, for blessings and overflow. I worship You. In Jesus' name I pray, amen.

AUTHORITY TO COMMAND THE HAND OF GOD

Commanding the hand of God is a very effective weapon to use in spiritual warfare. Generally, most people think that the phrase "the hand of God" refers to God's presence. Certainly, in some cases, it may; but the Bible reveals that it may also signify God's power expressed through judgment and blessings.

The hand of God simply means His power. Anytime you see the phrase "the hand of God," you should picture the power of God being *evident*. Acts 11:21 says, *"And **the hand of the Lord** was with them, and a great number believed and turned to the Lord."* This is a great example of the power of God being poured out, with the result that many people were saved.

When God's hand is at work in obvious ways, there will always be judgment against the adversaries and blessing toward the believers. In Acts 13:6–12, we read the story of Bar-Jesus, a sorcerer who was a fraud and full of deceit, knowingly twisting and perverting God's Word. Finally, Paul declared to him, *"The **hand of the Lord** is upon you, and you shall be blind, not seeing the sun for a time"* (Acts 13:11).

When the hand of the Lord was in evidence in this account, we see that blessing was on the apostles. As a result, *"the proconsul believed when he saw what had been done, being astonished at the teaching of the Lord"* (Acts 13:12). When Bar-Jesus was temporarily blinded, it was a sign and wonder, and the proconsul was astonished at the *power* of the teaching. By contrast, Bar-Jesus, the enemy of righteousness, was the recipient of God's judgment.

It is evident that declaring, or commanding, the hand of the Lord was a New Testament practice that brought incredible results. As believers, we have been given authority to command the hand of God. God gives His permission in Isaiah 45:11: *"Thus says the LORD, the Holy One of Israel, and his Maker: 'Ask Me of things to come concerning My sons; and concerning the work of My hands, **you command Me.**'"*

In other words, God is asking us to tell Him what we want, and promising to see to it that it is performed according to His Word. This is another aspect of our authority as believers. If evil spirits are harassing and assaulting us, then we can request that the hand of the Lord be outstretched to stop the demonic activity and bring restoration to us.

When the hand of the Lord gets involved in troubled situations, there will be compensation for one and judgment for another. Make sure that you are the one being compensated! When you command God's hand over the situations in your life, the thief is judged, and he has to compensate you sevenfold for all that he has stolen from you. (See Proverbs 6:31.)

Commanding Declaration

Satan, you are my adversary. You're the thief. You're the one who has stolen from me. In the name of Jesus, by the instruction of the Word of God and by the revelation of the Holy Spirit, I command the work of God's hand against you. The Word of God declares that when the hand of the Lord is in manifestation, no one can restrain it. (See Isaiah 14:27.) So, I declare: "The hand of the Lord be against you, satan."

Commanding Prayer

Father God, I ask You to stretch forth Your hand against the adversary of my life [specify finances, health, marriage, relationships, etc.]. According to Isaiah 45:11, I commission You to punish and penalize the devil for what he has put me through.

Thank You, Father, for performing Your Word in this situation. In Jesus' name, amen.

IMMUNITY FROM THE DEVIL

The definition of *immunity* is: "1. the state of being immune from or insusceptible…2. the condition that permits either natural or acquired resistance to a disease…3. exemption from any natural or usual liability."[16]

Spiritual immunity does not imply that the enemy will not *attempt* to attack you and your loved ones; he will certainly do so until Jesus returns for us. However, if we are abiding *in Christ* and consistently speaking God's Word in faith, his attempts to assault us will bounce off like darts on a shield.

You have effective authority over satan and his evil spirits *to the extent that* you submit to God and resist the devil. Satan and his demons cannot hurt you when you walk in your God-given authority.

Jesus told His disciples, "*I have given you authority to trample on snakes and scorpions and to overcome all the power of the enemy; nothing will harm you*" (Luke 10:19 NIV). And the apostle Paul exhors us to "[take] *the shield of faith with which you will be able to quench all the fiery darts of the wicked one*" (Ephesians 6:16). You

---

16. http://dictionary.reference.com.

can extinguish all of the flaming arrows of the evil one. You do not have to let even one arrow pierce you or your loved ones!

But *you* must take up the shield of faith; God will not take it up for you. *You* must exercise your will. *You* must pick it up and use it.

Immunity Is Not Automatic

There is no automatic immunity to the devil's schemes. Furthermore, all of God's promises are *conditional*. You cannot expect God to fulfill His promises to you unless you are doing what He requires of you. To put it bluntly, it doesn't matter how much "confessing and declaring" you do; if you are not abiding in Him continually, then you will not have immunity.

The word *continually* implies something that is practiced routinely, as a lifestyle. If sin is your lifestyle, then you do not have immunity to the devil's attacks! In fact, sin makes you even more susceptible to his assaults.

Speak Immunity

The key to exercising this immunity is your mouth. Your faith must be released through words. You must *say* that you are immune; you must *believe* that you are immune. Just as a vaccine makes you immune to a disease, so will believing in your heart, speaking the Word out loud, and meditating on that Word make you immune to the devil.

You can have immunity from the devil by believing and saying with your mouth: "I have immunity!" Your immunity will come as you renew your mind through the Word of God, thereby building your wall of protection.

Make these biblical affirmations to build your spiritual "immune system."

Declarations of Immunity

- The evil one cannot harm us nor steal from us, because the Lord keeps us safe.
- We are God's property! Satan has no hold on us.
- We've been marked with the seal of ownership by God Himself. (See 2 Corinthians 1:22.) He marked us with the Holy Spirit. We stand by faith in this truth.
- The Lord is our ark of safety. When we pass through the waters, the river will not overwhelm us or sweep us away. When we walk through the fire, we will not be burned, because the Lord is with us. (See Isaiah 43:2.) We will not fear, because He has redeemed us. He has called us by name. We belong to God.
- The blood of Jesus is over our lives, and the devil and his demons must pass over us! We live by the truth of the Word of God, and the truth is that He satisfies us with long life. (See Psalm 91:16.)
- We have entered the secret place, and the devil cannot find us, because we are covered with the blood of Jesus!
- A thousand may fall at our sides, even ten thousand at our right hand, but *no disaster will come near us!* (See Psalm 91:7.)
- We have made the Most High our dwelling, even our refuge, and so *no evil will befall us.* (See Psalm 91:1.)
- God rescues us and protects us, for we acknowledge His name, we are intimately acquainted with Him, and we love Him with all our heart, soul, mind, and strength. (See Deuteronomy 6:5; Matthew 22:37; Mark 12:30; Luke 10:27.)
- "*I will say of the* Lord, '*He is my refuge and my fortress; my God, in Him I will trust*'" (Psalm 91:2).

YOUR TONGUE PREDICTS YOUR FUTURE

Do you realize that you can predict your future? All you have to do is listen to your words. If you want to know the outlook of your health, what your finances will look like, and the future of your relationships, listen carefully to the words you are saying. If you do not like the future they are predicting, change what you are saying! Change your words, change your future!

OVERCOME ADVERSITY

"People may not deserve the destruction the devil brings them, but the devil doesn't give people what they deserve; he does whatever he can get away with."
—Gloria Copeland

Did you know that every battle you go through really matters to God? Your battle may not be your choice, but winning is!

You see, you will always have an enemy—satan, lucifer, the devil—but God anticipated the attacks of the enemy against you, and that's why He provided the cross!

The devil and his demons carefully plan attacks against you, and they fully intend for you to fail and be defeated. But Jesus shed His precious blood on the cross, to ensure your victory and recovery!

You see, satan despises God and hates anyone who receives God's affection. Satan comes against you because you are a potential source of pleasure to God. *"For [God] hast created all things, and for [His] pleasure they are and were created"* (Revelation 4:11 KJV).

Satan's real enemy is God. But, because he is powerless against God, he attacks that which is closest to the heart of God—you and me!

Satan's main purpose of warfare against you is to separate you from God. Since he couldn't stop you from getting born again, the next best thing is to keep you from having a relationship with God.

How does he go about fulfilling this goal? He assaults you with adversity, tests, trials, and constant pressure. He knows that if he can keep you down and discouraged, then you pose no real threat to him.

BEARING UP UNDER THE "SIFTING PROCESS"

This constant pressure is what Jesus referred to as the "sifting process."

> *And the Lord said, "Simon, Simon! Indeed, satan has asked for you, that he may sift you as wheat. But I have prayed for you, that your faith will not fail; and when you have returned to Me, strengthen your brethren."* (Luke 22:31–32)

In other words, Jesus told Peter, "When you have come through the battle victorious, you must use your victory to help others." The *Message* Bible puts it this way: *"Simon, stay on your toes. Satan has tried his best to separate all of you from me...I've prayed for you in particular that you not give in or give out."*

You must never say, "I can't take it anymore"! If you do, then satan knows he has almost accomplished his mission against you, and he will definitely see to it that you get more adversity, trials, and constant pressure. The devil knows that with a little more pressure, it is just a matter of time before you turn your back on God.

You see, the devil wants you to doubt God's integrity and thereby grieve His heart. But you must stand firm on the Word of God in Numbers 23:19 (CEV): *"God is no mere human! He doesn't* tell lies or change His mind. God always keeps his promises." God absolutely cannot lie, but satan is a liar—in fact, he is the "*father of lies*" (John 8:44 NIV)! So, you must learn how to fight your battle against him—no one else can do it for you! Most Christians do not know they have to fight the enemy every day.

You may have grown weary of standing. You may hope that things will get better, but it seems as if they're only getting worse. Perhaps satan has convinced you that this "faith stuff" doesn't really work. He may even be telling you that it doesn't do any good to speak the Word and do things God's way. The devil is hoping that you will eventually fall for these lies. He's hoping that the "sifting" will work and he will succeed in breaking you down.

No wonder Jesus warned Peter about this, saying, "*Simon, stay on your toes….*" In other words, you must stay alert and be on guard at all times! You see, the devil plans to wreak as much havoc as he can in your life, even to the point of killing you. But he cannot succeed if you will only use your God-given authority!

You cannot afford to get lax in your faith or to allow doubt and unbelief to steal your victory. Keep your foot on the devil's neck by boldly proclaiming the Word of God, never wavering in your faith. Declare, "*It is written…*" in every situation, and *do not quit* until you see the manifestation of your prayers.

"SUBJECT TO CHANGE!"

This single phrase can change your life. Second Corinthians 4:18 (KJV) says, "*We look not at the things which are seen, but at the things which are not seen:* **for the things which are seen are temporal; but the things which are not seen are eternal.**"

In his book *In the Footsteps of a Prophet*, Jerry Savelle relates that God once told him, "Things which are seen are temporal. If you can see it, then it's temporal. Another meaning for the word *temporal* is 'subject to change!'"[17]

Substituting the phrase "subject to change" for *"temporal"* in 2 Corinthians 4:18, we see that it reads, *"…for the things which are seen are **subject to change**"*!

The *Amplified Bible* expands the word *"temporal"* in this verse, adding the terms *"brief and fleeting."* Anything temporal—of this earth—is brief, fleeting, and subject to change. While it may be a fact to our five physical senses, it is *temporal*; therefore, it can be changed! No matter what the devil throws at us, it is *subject to change*! But the outcome is up to us, depending on whether we accept the situation or command it to change.

Second Corinthians 4:18 says that we should not even consider the things that are temporary. We should not believe the things we experience with our five physical senses—the things we see, feel, hear, touch, or smell. Rather, we are to consider the *unseen*—the things we believe God for, even when we have yet to see the manifestation of them. The realm of the unseen includes God's kingdom benefits, which are eternal and everlasting—benefits such as redemption, deliverance, health and healing, protection, rescue, prosperity, and provision.

Truth Trumps Facts

How do you know whether something is temporal or eternal? Ask yourself this question: "Can you find it in heaven?" If "yes," it is eternal; if "no," it is temporal.

Take sickness, for example. Is there sickness in heaven? No! Therefore, sickness is temporal!

---
17. Jerry Savelle, *In the Footsteps of a Prophet* (Crowley, TX: Savelle Publications, 1999).

What about lack? Is there any of that in heaven? No! So, lack is temporal, too.

Something may be a fact, in the natural; but that does not make it *the truth*. If it does not agree with the Word of God and what it says belongs to you, it is temporary and subject to change! If it is not resident in heaven, it can be changed on the earth.

- Sickness in your body? *Subject to change!*
- Trouble in your marriage? *Subject to change!*
- Checking account empty? *Subject to change!*
- Without a job? *Subject to change!*
- Broken relationships? *Subject to change!*
- Pain in your body? *Subject to change!*
- Unanswered prayers? *Subject to change!*

Whatever other people say is "impossible" is *subject to change*! If you really want your circumstances to change, then you must:

1. *Know the Word* that pertains to your situation,
2. *Believe and receive the Word*, in Jesus' name, and
3. *Speak that Word* sincerely, until the desired results manifest.

The truth of God's Word will always prevail over the "facts." Take cancer, for example—it's *temporal*! Although the doctor may say that you have cancer, that is not what the Word says! While it may be a fact (at this time), it's not *the* truth! It is always *subject to change*, as is all sickness and disease. Why? Because the Bible truth is this: "By the stripes laid on Jesus' back, you *were* healed!" (See 1 Peter 2:24.) The truth of the Word of God *always* trumps facts.

Every circumstance or situation in life is subject to change, if you are faithful to do what Jesus commanded in the following Scriptures:

For assuredly, I say to you, whoever says to this mountain, "Be removed and be cast into the sea," and does not doubt in his heart, but believes that those things he says will be done, he will have whatever he says. Therefore I say to you, whatever things you ask when you pray, believe that you receive them, and you will have them. (Mark 11:23–24)

If you have faith as a mustard seed, you can say to this mulberry tree, "Be pulled up by the roots and be planted in the sea," and it would obey you. (Luke 17:6)

If you abide in Me, and My words abide in you, you will ask what you desire, and it shall be done for you. (John 15:7)

In the time between when you believe you receive a promise from the Word and when it manifests in your life, keep looking at what the Word says, not at the circumstances, for we are to *"walk by faith, not by sight"* (2 Corinthians 5:7).

SUBJECT TO CHANGE!

We consider and look not to the things that are seen but to the things that are unseen; **for the things that are visible are temporal** [**subject to change**]. (2 Corinthians 4:18 AMP)

God…gives life to the dead and speaks of the nonexistent things that [He has foretold and promised] as if they [already] existed. (Romans 4:17 AMP)

We can change our circumstances by speaking the Word of God. Jesus did, and so can you! Call into manifestation the things that are not (yet!), and they will *replace* what presently exists!

The following table is an exercise that can help believers speak truth into their circumstances. Follow these simple guidelines:

1. In the first column of the table below, list the "seen" things—the problems you are presently facing.
2. In the second column, list the "unseen" things—the desired outcomes of these problems.
3. Refer to the contents page to locate specific topics that address your problems. Find at least two Scriptures/declarations for each problem and write them in the second column, along with the corresponding page numbers, like in the example below. You might also want to flag these pages for easy access when you need to refer to them.
4. On a separate sheet of paper, write a prayer by personalizing the Scriptures and declarations.
5. Pray this prayer aloud several times a day until you receive revelation knowledge about your situation. Believe and speak the Word until the manifestation comes. Do not quit!

X   O
PRESENTLY EXISTS   DESIRED OUTCOME

WHAT IS SEEN (the "facts" of your current situation)	WHAT IS UNSEEN (the truth of God's Word)
EX: Diagnosed with cancer	EX: NEED HEALING IN BODY a. Health & Healing b. Principles of Sowing & Reaping c. Power of the Blood of Jesus

WHAT IS SEEN (the "facts" of your current situation)	WHAT IS UNSEEN (the truth of God's Word)
1.	a. _____ b. _____ c. _____
2.	a. _____ b. _____ c. _____
3.	a. _____ b. _____ c. _____

Speak to the Mountain

A mountain is any obstacle or hindrance standing in the way of God's perfect will in your life. A mountain is something that seems too big for you—something that seems impossible to surmount, such as cancer or financial debt. Jesus instructed us on how we should handle a mountain:

> *Whoever says to this mountain, "Be lifted up and thrown into the sea," and does not doubt at all in his heart but believes that what he says will take place, it will be done for him.*
>
> (Mark 11:23)

The words you speak are a key factor in activating your faith. Authority is released when you speak God's Word. As Don Gossett has said, "Your mountain needs to hear your voice!" You see, your mountain *will* respond to your voice.

If you want to see results when you pray, you will have to use your voice to change your situation. In fact, if you truly understood what was on the other side of your mountain, you would not delay—you would shout to your mountain, "Move out of the way!"

No Camping Allowed!

> DO NOT DELAY! SHOUT TO THE MOUNTAIN, "MOVE OUT OF THE WAY!"

Too many people want to camp out in the valley instead of moving the mountain out of the way. There are several reasons why people remain on the campsite: 1) Some have gotten used to going from one crisis to another; they would not know what to do if there were not some kind of drama going on all the time; 2) some are unaware that they can move the mountain; 3) some try to go *around* the mountain, but it is a long way around it, so they grow weary and give up; and 4) others are simply lazy or apathetic. You see, this walk of faith takes effort. It is hard work, and it requires perseverance!

Refuse to give in to the temptation of speaking before you think. Refuse to speak how your body feels or what your emotions are trying to tell you. Refuse to speak wrong words when you are in pain or are frustrated or angry. Put a guard over your mouth. (See Psalm 141:3.)

You cannot move the mountain by thinking about it, nor can you *will* the mountain to move. Jesus said to *speak* to the mountain. Notice how your mouth plays a huge role in moving the mountain. Following is an example of how to speak to your mountain.

Mountain-Moving Declaration

You mountain of _____ [sickness, disease, debt, lack, strife, etc.], trying to exalt yourself above the Word of God—I speak to you and tell you to be removed, right now! Jesus said you would obey me, so go now, in Jesus' name!

I have faith in God! I say to this mountain of _____ , "Be removed and be cast into the sea." I do not doubt in my heart; I believe it is done. I have what I say. I agree with Jesus—whatever things I ask for when I pray, I believe that I receive them. I have them now! And I forgive anyone whom I've held anything against. In Jesus' name, amen.

Mountain-Moving Confession

I speak to every mountain that has hindered supernatural increase in my life, and command it to move. I am ready to receive God's blessings for me!

According to Jesus' very own words in Mark 11:22–25, this is how to answer every challenge that comes into your life.

USE YOUR WORDS TO CREATE

In his book *Faith and Confession*, Charles Capps reports that Jesus told him, "I have told My people they can have what they say, but My people are saying what they have."[18] You must learn to speak the desired result according to the Word of God, not to report the way things appear to your natural senses.

---
18. Charles Capps, *Faith and Confession* (Tulsa, OK: Harrison House, Inc., 1987).

Confession works in everything—good *or* bad! The law of confession works not only for salvation (getting saved) but also for everything else in life. In fact, in the New Testament, the word for *"salvation"* is generally *soteria* (so-tay-REE-ah), which literally means "deliverance, preservation, soundness, prosperity, happiness, rescue, general well-being."[19]

In light of that, consider Luke 19:9: *"Today salvation has come to this house."* Substitute any of the synonyms for salvation, and this verse becomes a real eye-opener! "Today deliverance has come to this house"; "Today safety (protection from harm) has come to this house"; "Today health has come to this house." Do you see how believers have shorted themselves on all of the benefits of God's will, expressed in His Word?

Proverbs 6:2 (NIV) says, *"You have been trapped by what you said, ensnared by the words of your mouth."* Confess sickness and poverty, and you'll have them! Confess health, prosperity, and sound relationships, and you'll have them! The choice is yours.

> WORDS ACTIVATE FAITH LIKE VINEGAR ACTIVATES BAKING SODA.

Confess what the Word of God says about you and your situation, even if you are not convinced of it right away, because *"faith comes by hearing, and hearing by the word of God"* (Romans 10:17). Confess the Word often enough, with sincerity, and, sooner or later, faith will drop into your heart as you hear the Word of God on your own lips. Then, you'll have whatever you have believed in your heart and confessed with your mouth. (See Mark 11:23.)

---

19. Strong's #G4991.

Confessions of Breakthrough

- Heavenly Father, I see that it is through Your Word that we have access to wisdom, knowledge, and understanding. So, I covenant with You to always give voice to Your Word. I will not allow my voice to speak the words of the enemy. I will give him no place in my life. Instead, I give place to Your Word and Your Spirit.

- I boldly proclaim that we are redeemed from the curse of the law. We are delivered from the authority of darkness and have been translated into the kingdom of Your dear Son. In our pathway are life, healing, and prosperity, for Abraham's blessings are ours! (See Galatians 3:13–14.)

- The Greater One dwells in us, and we have made Your Word our foundation. Therefore, we will not fall; neither shall we fail. A thousand may fall at our sides, and ten thousand at our right hands, but the enemy shall not approach us, for You have given Your angels charge over us; they keep us in all our ways. Christ has redeemed us from poverty, sickness, and spiritual death. Therefore, I boldly confess that we are the redeemed of the Lord! (See Psalm 91:7, 11.)

- Heavenly Father, because of Your Word, I forbid any sickness or disease to operate in our bodies. Our bodies are the temples of the Holy Ghost. (See 1 Corinthians 6:19.)

- We will proclaim with our mouths, *"Christ has redeemed us from the curse of the law"* (Galatians 3:13), and *"[Christ] who Himself bore our sins in His own body on the tree, that we, having died to sins, might live for righteousness; by whose stripes you were healed"* (1 Peter 2:24). Your Word is transforming our bodies, because You sent Your Word (Jesus!) and healed and delivered us from all our destructions. (See Psalm 107:20.)

- Father, Your Word is transforming our bodies, causing growths to disappear and sicknesses to flee. Every cell, organ, and tissue functions perfectly, just exactly the way that God designed it to function. Our bones and joints function properly, in Jesus' name! The Spirit of God is upon us, and the Word of God is within us.

+ Therefore, we will fear no evil, for Your Word and Your Spirit comfort us. We are far from oppression; fear does not come near us. No weapon formed against us will prosper, but whatever we do will prosper! This is our heritage given to us of the Lord and our righteousness is of Him! (See Isaiah 54:14, 17; Psalm 1:3.)

+ Heavenly Father, I resolve to speak only Your Word, so that the Holy Spirit within us will guide us into all truth. I see these things belong to us. I proclaim that they are ours.

+ I declare that we will not be deceived, and the enemy will not steal what You have given us. I boldly declare that we walk in prosperity and in health, for Your Word abides within us. The Greater One is in us, and He will put us over.

+ Even though many may fall by our sides, I will continue to proclaim that the enemy shall not come near us. I release the angels and the ministering spirits, and charge them with Your Word to garrison about our homes, our vehicles, our workplaces, our families, and our finances, and to guide us with the wisdom of God. You keep us safe because our minds are stayed on You. Thank You, Father; thank You, Jesus!

+ I confess that we have perfect knowledge of every situation. We do not want for the wisdom of God, for we have the mind of Christ. We have overcome the world, the flesh, and the devil, because the Greater One is in us! (See 1 Corinthians 2:16; 1 John 4:4.)

In Jesus' precious name, I declare these things. Amen!

GUARD YOUR JOY!

The book *If Satan Can't Steal Your Joy, He Can't Keep Your Goods* by Dr. Jerry Savelle has had a powerful impact on me. The sad fact is that we have all been robbed by satan, at one time or another, whether he stole material goods (property, money, jobs, and so on) or less tangible things, such as our health, relationships, ministry efforts, peace, and joy. How is he able to do it?

When satan attacks us, we are too quick to get depressed and discouraged. Then, we usually open our big mouth, complain, and speak words that are in direct opposition to the Word of God. In so doing, we let the devil walk off with our stuff!

Many of us just hand over our stuff to the devil without a fight. Now, unless we force him to give it back, according to Mark 3:27, he'll keep it indefinitely! No amount of whining will make him feel sorry for you or prompt him to give back your health, put money back in your bank account, or fix your marriage!

Do not be naive; the words that come out of your mouth in response to the attack determines if the devil can keep your goods! Consider this: The Word of God produces *joy*—and no man can take away your joy. Only *you* can give it up! (See John 16:22.)

Joy has a voice. What does it say? *"Praise the LORD of hosts, for the LORD is good, for His mercy endures forever"* (Jeremiah 33:11). Remember, a voice is audible.

You cannot be defeated as long as you still have your *joy*. Habakkuk 3:18 says, *"Yet I will rejoice."* The devil doesn't know what to do when he has launched an attack against you, and you just keep on praising the Lord! Don Gossett says the devil is allergic to praise; so, make him miserable by sincerely saying "praise the Lord" ten times, and get back your joy. Then, speak the Word and demand the devil give your stuff back!

NUCLEAR WEAPONS FOR ELIMINATING ADVERSITY

- Renew your mind! You must know and speak the Word of God. Study your Bible and learn what God has to say about your situation. Use this *Spiritual Weapons Handbook* to help you find the Scriptures that fit your situation, and then declare His Word boldly! (See Romans 12:2; Hebrews 4:12.)

- Speak to the mountain! Jesus spoke to demons and natural forces, and so can you!

- Speak only what God's Word says about your situation. *"Death and life are in the power of the tongue…"* (Proverbs 18:21). You must find out what God says and only say what He says. Do not be double-minded!

- Take your authority over satan in the name of Jesus. Tell him "no" and kick him out of your affairs. (See Luke 10:19; Philippians 2:9–10.)

- Put on the armor of God every day. (See Ephesians 6:13–18.)

- Seek the wisdom of a spiritual mentor. (See Proverbs 1:5.) To avoid confusion, however, you should consult with only one mature Christian (two at the most). Learn to hear from God for yourself!

- Do not glorify the works of the devil by complaining incessantly to others about your battle.

- Do not give up! Faith and patience are the "power twins"! You must exercise both principles in order to overcome adversity.

INVOKE THE BLOOD OF JESUS

"The blood of Jesus doesn't become less effective when the devil fights hard. The power of the resurrection doesn't lessen in the heat of circumstances. It's as strong today as it was the very day Jesus' body rose out of the grave over two thousand years ago."
—Jesse Duplantis

Many people do not understand the spiritual weapons God has provided to keep the devil under their feet. The Bible says. *"And they overcame him* [the devil] *by the blood of the Lamb and by the word of their testimony"* (Revelation 12:11). Speaking the Word of God and applying the blood of Jesus are highly effective spiritual weapons.

When you plead the blood of Jesus into any situation, the devil must bow to it. If there is even the slightest inkling that the devil will try to trespass on your territory, shout, "Behold the blood of Jesus, satan! Pass over and be gone!"

The blood of Jesus has power to meet every need you might have. Applying the blood is how you activate all of the promises of God. It is important to understand that the basis of all salvation, deliverance, and healing is the blood of God's covenant. Plainly,

Jesus said, "*This is My blood of the new covenant, which is shed for many for the remission of sins*" (Matthew 26:28).

Everything God has belongs to us, because we have a blood covenant through Jesus Christ. If we need wisdom, then God promises to give it to us. If we are weak, then He will be our Strength. If we lack anything, then God promises to provide it, because of the covenant we have with Him.

HONOR THE BLOOD

As Andrew Murray so aptly put it, "It is impossible for us to think too highly of, or to expect too much from, the power of Jesus' blood."[20] Did you ever stop to think that the name of Jesus wouldn't work if it weren't for the blood? For that reason, it is imperative that we make much of the blood of Jesus.

There is much power available in the blood. Where the blood of Jesus is honored, the Holy Spirit is attentive and eager to help. Believing in and honoring the blood of Jesus releases the power for provision. When you respect the blood of the Lamb, heaven immediately moves on your behalf.

You must have faith in the blood of Jesus and in what it can do for you. You activate your faith by speaking the Word of God concerning what the blood has accomplished for you. Declare the statements below as you honor the blood of Jesus:

Declarations to Honor the Blood of Jesus

- Father God, I honor the blood of Jesus. I am so very grateful for the power available through the blood.
- Thank You, Jesus, that You shed Your precious blood so that I could overcome every attack of the enemy.

---

20. Andrew Murray, *The Power of the Blood of Jesus* (New Kensington, PA: Whitaker House, 1993), 31.

- Through the blood of Jesus, I have been redeemed out of the hands of the devil.
- Thank You, Father, that as I walk in the light, the blood of Jesus cleanses me from all sins.
- Through the blood of Jesus, I have the life of God in me. Holy Spirit, give me revelation knowledge of that truth.
- Thank You, Father, that through the blood of Jesus, I have access to the presence of God.

Declarations to Activate the Blood of Jesus

- Thank You, Father, for the benefits and provisions of the blood of Jesus.
- I stand on the authority of the blood of Jesus to proclaim victory over sin, satan, and his agents!
- I paralyze all satanic oppressors delegated against me with the blood of Jesus.
- Devil, you cannot put any sickness or disease on me, because I am redeemed by the blood of the Lamb!
- Devil, look at the blood of Jesus! The One who shed His blood crushed your head (see Genesis 3:15 NIV), and He is my Lord!
- Father, let the blood of Jesus speak confusion into the camp of the enemy. Their plans and schemes will come to naught.

APPLY THE BLOOD

It is not enough that you know you have a covenant with God; you must *purposely* apply the blood of Jesus over your life and your loved ones, just as the Israelites had to do to their doorposts during the first Passover.

> *They shall take some of the blood and put it on the two doorposts and on the lintel of the houses....Now the blood shall be a sign for you on the houses where you are. And when I see the blood, I will pass over you; and the plague shall not be on you to destroy you....And you shall take a bunch of hyssop, dip it in the blood that is in the basin, and strike the lintel and the two doorposts with the blood that is in the basin. And none of you shall go out of the door of his house until morning.*
> (Exodus 12:7, 13, 22)

> WHEN THE BLOOD HAS BEEN APPLIED, WE CANNOT BE DENIED!

The Israelites had to *do* something to apply the blood, and so do we! Unlike the Israelites, we do not physically apply blood to our homes, vehicles, or loved ones. Instead of using a bunch of hyssop to apply physical blood, we symbolically use our tongues and speak the Word of God in faith. Our authority and protection are in the blood of Jesus and the Word of God that comes out of our mouths.

Satan and his demons are out to destroy us, but we can defend ourselves, our families, and our possessions with the precious blood of the Lord Jesus Christ. (See Revelation 12:11.) It is your responsibility to put the blood on your life! How do you do it? By following these steps:

1. Say out loud: "Devil, you may try to threaten me/us/_____, but I apply the blood of Jesus to myself/us/_____/this situation, and instantly stop every demonic force. The blood of Jesus is against you, devil, and we overcome you by saying, 'It is written...'!"

2. Search the Bible, with the help of this book and/or a concordance, for Scriptures pertaining to your situation.

3. Boldly speak those Scriptures aloud. Doing so will build your faith, but it also informs the devil that you know your rights as a believer, and you will enforce them! Just as importantly, speaking the Word of God activates the angels to perform that Word on your behalf.

Declaration to Apply the Blood of Jesus

In the name of Jesus, I apply the blood of Jesus over _____ (names) today. I apply the blood of Jesus over every area of our lives. I apply the blood of Jesus over our jobs and businesses and ministries. I apply the blood of Jesus to our relationships. I apply the blood of Jesus over our homes and our vehicles—anywhere and everywhere we are. I apply the precious blood of Jesus to our ears, thumbs, and toes (see Leviticus 8:23–24), knowing that the blood cleanses and sanctifies all that enters into our ears, everything we put our hands to do, and wherever our feet take us in the course of our duties today. I declare by faith that this is the blood that seals our covenant with God! (See Zechariah 9:11–12.) Father, I know that when the blood has been applied, we cannot be denied!

PLEAD THE BLOOD

Another way to place the blood on your life and those of your loved ones is to plead the blood of Jesus. The term "plead" is a legal term. For example, a lawyer may plead a case. He pleads not in the sense of "begging" but in the sense of *claiming his client's rights*.

> **THE BLOOD OF JESUS MAKES YOU RADIOACTIVE TO THE DEVIL. DRAW YOUR "SAFE PERIMETER" AND WARN HIM TO STAY OUT!**

In the court of heaven, the blood of Jesus is our witness; the job of a witness is to speak! Hebrews 12:24 tells us that the blood of Jesus speaks: *"The blood of sprinkling... speaks better things than that of Abel."*

The blood of Abel cried out for vengeance, but the blood of Jesus speaks mercy, peace, pardon, and reconciliation for all who are bound by satan.

Kenneth W. Hagin explains it very well: "The blood speaks of who we are and what we have because of Jesus' shed blood....Pleading the blood is *activating* what happened through the blood of Jesus Christ on the cross. It's asking God to provide for us what Jesus' blood has already purchased. It is a statement of faith about what happened at Calvary."[21]

Every time the enemy comes to accuse you or tries to steal your redemptive benefits, you have a witness who will plead on your behalf—*the blood of Jesus*! Every time the accuser comes to harass and trouble you, you can shout, "I plead the blood of Jesus!" When you plead the blood, you are allowing the blood of Jesus to speak for and represent you. Our accuser has no case when we plead the blood.

The blood of Jesus gives you rights over the devil and rights with God! You claim your rights as a believer by believing and proclaiming the promises of God.

---

21. Kenneth W. Hagin, "The Blood Still Speaks," *Word of Faith* magazine (April 2011).

Pleading the blood daily gives protection *before* adversity strikes; it serves to prevent attacks from the adversary. Because we are in the very end of the end times, we must plead the blood of Jesus continuously. There is so much tragedy and disaster everywhere, but it cannot come near us or our loved ones if we are protected by the blood. Even though tragedy and disaster are rampant all around us, pleading the blood of Jesus sincerely and in faith will give us immunity against them.

HOLD THE BLOOD

You can also "hold" the blood against the devil until victory comes. Picture a hand stretched out like a police officer to stop him. Keep the blood applied; never release it until the devil flees! Too many people quit too soon.

SPRINKLE THE BLOOD

In Scripture, the blood is spoken of in two ways: blood shed and blood sprinkled.

Jesus said, *"This cup is the new testament in My blood, which is shed for you"* (Luke 22:20). We memorialize His sacrifice every time we observe the sacrament of Communion. But that is usually the limit of most Christians' knowledge of Jesus' blood. They know only about the blood being shed, not about its being sprinkled! *"The blood of sprinkling…speaks better things than that of Abel"* (Hebrews 12:24).

If Christ is Lord of your life, then the "doorposts" of your heart have been sprinkled by His blood. And this sprinkling is not for forgiveness only; it also brings protection, healing, soundness, and prosperity!

When you are sprinkled with the blood of Jesus, you are totally under the protection of Christ against all the destroying powers of satan. When his forces see Christ's blood on your doorposts, they must pass over you. They cannot touch you, because they cannot touch anyone who has been sprinkled with Christ's blood! (See Exodus 12.) The precious benefits of the blood extend far beyond forgiveness of sins.

The "blood of sprinkling" represents the pains, the sufferings, the humiliation, and the death that the Lord Jesus Christ He endured on the behalf of guilty mankind. Be a child of God who regularly practices the sprinkling of the blood of the Lord Jesus Christ, because this is the blood that seals our covenant with God! Sprinkle it anywhere there is evidence of sickness, pressure, lack, or any kind of satanic effort to thwart the complete will of God in Your life.

Declaration to Hold and Sprinkle the Blood of Jesus

> Father God, I hold the blood of Jesus against anything that could come against us. Father, I thank You that part of our covenant with You is Your promise to protect us. I plead the blood of Jesus as our Defense, and call the blood as the Witness to take the stand and testify on our behalf that Jesus paid the price on the cross. Jesus, sprinkle Your blood on us today. (See 1 Peter 1:2–3.)

DRAW A BLOOD LINE

You can also draw a blood line of protection around yourself, your home, and your loved ones. In Joshua 2:18, the scarlet cord is symbolic of the redemptive work of Christ that saves us all. Just as Rahab hung a *"line of scarlet cord in the window,"* so we, too, can symbolically hang or draw a blood line of protection around our lives.

I encourage you to draw a symbolic blood line of protection. Point your finger and "draw" a circle in the air around you and all your loved ones, your vehicles, your homes, and all your possessions, representing a blood line the enemy cannot cross.

Declaration to Draw a Blood Line

> Father, I remember the first Passover and how they took *"a lamb for a household"* (Exodus 12:3) and drew a blood line that stopped the destroyer. (See Exodus 12:22–23.) Jesus is our *"Lamb who was slain"* (Revelation 5:12), so, devil, you have to pass over us!
>
> (Point your index finger and symbolically draw a circle in the air around you and all your loved ones as you declare the following:)
>
> Just as Rahab hung the scarlet cord from her window as a sign of protection for all who were of her household and all their possessions (see Joshua 2:18–21; 6:23), so I draw a blood line of protection around each one of us and everything that concerns us. Although hard times may come to those around us, *they pass us by* because we are covered with the blood of Jesus and established in righteousness. (See Isaiah 54:14–15.)
>
> Father, I thank You that no power of hell can withstand the proclamation of the blood of Jesus! The Word says and the blood *does!*

WIELD THE BLOOD AS A WEAPON

As the blood of a human carries his life, so does the blood of Jesus carry the life of the Son of God. As we speak the word "blood," we must remember that the blood of Jesus carries all the power, Spirit, and life that are in Jesus.

Each time we say the word "blood" in faith, we are bringing the very life of Jesus to stand against the destroying power of satan. The blood of Jesus makes you *radioactive* to the devil! Draw your "safe perimeter," and warn him to stay out!

Additional Declarations to Apply, Plead, and Otherwise Activate the Blood

In the name of Jesus…

- I plead the blood of Jesus for my healing (or finances, etc).
- I apply the blood of Jesus to these symptoms.
- I believe I receive the manifestation of my healing through the blood of Jesus.
- I apply the blood of Jesus to every stubborn problem in my life.
- I sprinkle the blood of Jesus on _____.
- I resist you, evil spirits of _____ (sickness, financial lack, calamity, fear, etc.), with the blood of the Lamb.
- I draw a blood line around this place that the devil cannot cross. I declare, "Access denied!" (Think of a large flashing sign, like the Amber Alert signs on the interstates.)
- I draw the blood line of protection around me and my loved ones, our property, our identifications, all our animals, and all our possessions.

Part II: Nuclear Strategies to Blast the Devil 117

- I plead the blood of the Lord Jesus Christ against this situation/problem/sickness: _____.
- In the name of Jesus, I sprinkle the blood of Jesus over _____. Jesus, sprinkle Your blood on _____ (or on the situation).
- I apply the blood of Jesus to this problem/sickness, and bind its power to remain! There is power in Jesus' blood to set everything right, satan. Jesus' blood works now to remove every evil work!
- I hold the blood of Jesus against you, satan, and declare that it overcomes you, and you must flee now! (Continue to believe and to repeat this until every trace of this trouble or sickness is gone.)
- I hold the blood of Jesus as a shield against any power that is poised to harass and torment me or my loved ones.
- I hold the blood of Jesus against any demonic delay of my miracles.
- The blood of Jesus makes us *immune* to the attacks of the enemy! (See "Declarations of Immunity" on page ##.)
- The devil may try to threaten us, but he will find no opportunity for his acts of terrorism against any of us!
- I boldly declare: "It happens for us, just as it happened for the children of Israel: the destroyer—the devil—must pass over us!"

THE WORST DAY OF THE DEVIL'S LIFE

Kenneth E. Hagin summarizes the effect the blood of Jesus has on our enemy, the devil: "If you want to see satan run, begin talking about the blood of Jesus. You see, he remembers what happened when that blood was shed. The devil thought he had it made. He thought he had captured Jesus, the Son of God. He thought he had thwarted God's plan. But during those three days in hell, Jesus took back the keys of hell and death. (See Revelation 1:18.) He disarmed the powers and principalities and made a public spectacle of them. (See Colossians 2:15 NIV.) And instead of being held captive by the forces of darkness, Jesus ascended into heaven. The blood of Jesus is the power that destroyed all the works of the enemy!"[22]

---

22. Hagin, "Blood Still Speaks."

DECLARE THE BLESSING

Contrary to what many people believe, or have heard through traditional teaching, the blessing of God is not a material item, such as a house or a car. While these things are some *results* of the blessing, they are not the blessing itself. The blessing is an empowerment or enablement from God to help you get supernatural results in everything you do.

Whether in your job, your ministry, your relationships, your gifts, or something else with which God has endowed you, when the blessing is in operation, you can't fail! When you speak God's Word, you release the blessing.

Declaring Scriptures and biblical affirmations such as those included in this section will not only increase your faith; it will also activate the angels. Hebrews 1:14 tells us, *"Are* [angels] *not all ministering spirits sent forth to minister for those who will inherit salvation?"* Also, Psalm 103:20 says that angels heed the voice of the Lord, doing His commands. So, when we speak the Word out loud, the angels are activated to bring that promise to pass for us.

Remember, we should never pray to angels or worship them. Simply abiding in God and speaking His Word with sincerity will put them to work.

DECLARE THE BLESSING OVER YOUR FAMILY

Scriptural Assurances of God's Blessing for the Family

Blessed shall you be when you come in, and **blessed** shall you be when you go out. The LORD will cause your enemies who rise against you to be defeated before your face; they shall come out against you one way and flee before you seven ways. The LORD will command **the blessing** on you in your storehouses and in all to which you set your hand, and He will **bless** you in the land which the LORD your God is giving you.
(Deuteronomy 28:6–8)

Your [Abraham's] descendants shall be as the dust of the earth; you shall spread abroad to the west and the east, to the north and the south; and in you and in your seed all the families of the earth shall be **blessed**. (Genesis 28:14)

Blessed be the God and Father of our Lord Jesus Christ, who has [already] **blessed** us with every spiritual **blessing** in the heavenly places in Christ. (Ephesians 1:3)

The blessing of the LORD [always!] makes one rich, and He adds no sorrow with it. (Proverbs 10:22)

Declarations of God's Blessing for the Family

- Thank You, Lord, that the blessing is working in us, on us, and around us. I declare that we are blessed when we come in and blessed when we go out. Jesus came to the earth to restore the blessing that Adam lost in the garden of Eden when he sinned;

and because we are children of God, we have a covenant right to the blessing!

- I declare that, like Abraham, we are blessed to be a blessing, until all families of the earth are blessed. (See Genesis 12:1–3.) Because the blessing of God is on our lives, we are empowered to prosper in every endeavor that we take on and every project that we begin!

- We are blessed on our jobs, in our businesses, and in our investments; our ministries and all our relationships are blessed! Those in authority over us will see the blessing of God on our lives, as they did on the life of Joseph, and we have favor as a result!

- Thank You, Lord, for blessing us with all spiritual blessings in heavenly places. We are mighty, healthy, wealthy, influential, and blessed! In Jesus' name, I declare that it is so!

Declarations of God's Blessing for Children

- I declare and decree that our children honor and obey their parents in the Lord as His representatives, because this is just and right. My child(ren), _____, honor, esteem, and value their parents as precious, for this is the first commandment with a promise: that all may be well with them, and that they may live long on the earth. (See Ephesians 6:1–3.)

- As parents, we will not provoke, irritate, or frustrate our children. We will not be hard on them or harass them; cause them to become discouraged, sullen, or morose; or make them feel inferior and fretful. We will not break or wound their spirits, but we will rear them tenderly in the training, discipline, counsel, and admonition of the Lord. We will train them in the way they should go, and when they are old, they will not depart from it. In Jesus' name, amen. (See Ephesians 6:4; Proverbs 22:6.)

+ Father, in the name of Jesus, I pray and confess Your Word over our child(ren), _____, and surround them with my faith—faith in Your Word that You watch over it to perform it!

+ I confess and believe that my child(ren),_____, is/are disciple(s) of Christ, taught of the Lord, and obedient to Your will. Great is their peace and undisturbed composure. They are established in righteousness and far from oppression. They will not fear, and neither shall terror come near them. (See Isaiah 54:13–14 AMP.) You, O God, contend with those who contend with _____. You give them safety and ease them.

+ Father, You will perfect that which concerns us. Our children concern us; we commit and cast the care of them, once and for all, over on You, Father. They are in Your hands, and we are positively persuaded that You are able to guard and keep that which we have committed to You. (See 2 Timothy 1:12.)

+ I believe and confess that my child(ren), _____, choose life and love You, Lord. They obey Your voice and cling to You; for You are their life and the length of their days. (See Proverbs 3:2.) I believe and confess that You give Your angels charge over _____, to accompany and defend and preserve them in all their ways. You, Lord, are their Refuge and Fortress. The enemy is turned back from them, in the name of Jesus! They increase in wisdom and in favor with God and man.

+ Father God, I declare and decree that, according to Deuteronomy 6:2, 5, my child(ren), _____, reverently fear the Lord and keep all His statutes and His commandments. They love the Lord their God with all their mind, heart, and might—with their entire being. They are the head and not the tail; they shall be above only, not beneath, because they heed the commandments of the Lord their God and are watchful to do them. They are blessed when they come in and blessed when they go out. (See Deuteronomy 28:6, 13.)

+ I declare that my child(ren), _____, make(s) right choices according to the Word of God. (See Isaiah 54:13.) They have Christian friends, and they will make no friendship with an angry man; with a furious man, my child(ren) will not go, lest they learn his ways and fall into a snare. (See Proverbs 22:24–25.) I pray that my child(ren) will walk with the wise and become wise, and that they will never keep the companionship of fools and thereby be destroyed. (See Proverbs 13:20.)

+ God has set aside a Christian wife or husband for each of my children; they shall never be unequally yoked with unbelievers. (See 1 Corinthians 15:33; 2 Corinthians 6:14.) They walk and live habitually in the Holy Spirit, responsive to and controlled and guided by the Spirit. (See Galatians 5:16 AMP.)

+ In the name of Jesus, I pray that my child(ren), _____, will speak the same thing, and that there be no division among them, but that they will be perfectly joined together in the same mind and in the same judgment. (See 1 Corinthians 1:10.)

+ We rejoice greatly that we find our child(ren), _____, walking in truth. (See 2 John 1:4.) They have the spirit of wisdom and revelation—of insight into mysteries and secrets—in the deep and intimate knowledge of God. Their eyes have been flooded with Light, so that they can know and understand the hope to which He has called them, and how rich is His glorious inheritance in the saints. (See Ephesians 1:17–18 AMP.)

Prayer for a Teenager

Father, in the name of Jesus, I affirm Your Word over my teenager. I commit him/her to You and delight myself also in You. I thank You that You deliver _____ out of rebellion and into right relationship with his/her parents.

Father, the first commandment with a promise is to the child who obeys his parents in the Lord. You said that all will be well with him and that he will live long on the earth. I affirm this promise on behalf of my child, asking You to give him/her an obedient spirit, that he/she may honor—esteem and value as precious—those in right authority over him/her.

Father, forgive me for mistakes I made out of my own unresolved hurts or selfishness that may have caused my teenager hurt. I release the anointing that is upon Jesus to bind up and heal our broken hearts. Give us the ability to understand and forgive one another, as God for Christ's sake has forgiven us. Thank You for the Holy Spirit, who leads us into all truth and corrects erroneous perceptions about past and present situations.

Thank You for teaching us to listen to each other and for giving my teenager an ear that hears admonition, for then he/she will be called wise. I affirm that I will speak excellent and princely things, and the opening of my lips shall be for right things. Father, I commit to train and teach my teenager in the way that he/she is to go, so that when he/she is old, he/she will not depart from sound doctrine and teaching but will follow it all the days of his/her life. In the name of Jesus, I command rebellion to be far from the heart of my teenager and confess that he/she is willing and obedient, free to enjoy the reward of Your promises. He/she shall be peaceful, bringing peace to others.

Father, according to Your Word, we have been given the ministry of reconciliation, and I release this ministry and the word of reconciliation into this family situation. I refuse to provoke or irritate or fret my child. I will not be hard on him/her, lest he/she become discouraged, feeling inferior and frustrated. I will not break his/her spirit, in the name of Jesus, and by the power of the Holy Spirit. Father, I forgive my teenager for the wrongs which he/she has done, and I stand in the gap until he/she comes to his/her senses and escapes out of the snare of the enemy, which is rebellion.

Thank You for watching over Your Word to perform it, turning and reconciling the heart of my teenager to the parents and the hearts of the parents to the child. Thank You for bringing my teenager back into a healthy relationship with You and with me, that our lives might glorify You! In Jesus' name, amen. (See Ezekiel 22:30; Malachi 4:6; Jeremiah 1:12; Isaiah 1:19; 54:13; 61:1; John 14:6; 20:23; Ephesians 6:1–3; Psalm 37:4; Proverbs 8:6–7; 13:1; 22:6.)

DECLARE THE BLESSING OF ABUNDANCE

The following prayers and tools will help you to receive God's promises of abundance and success. Step out in faith and boldly declare that God will cause you and your family members to prosper!

Declarations of Prosperity and Provision

- I boldly declare, "We are the uncompromisingly righteous; therefore, we shall flourish like a palm tree [long-lived, stately, upright, useful, and fruitful]; we shall grow like a cedar [majestic, stable, durable, and incorruptible]. We are planted in the house of the Lord, and we flourish in the courts of our God. Growing in grace and favor, we shall continue to bring forth fruit, even in old age. We are full of spiritual vitality and rich in the abundance of trust, love, and contentment. We are living memorials to show that the Lord is upright and faithful to His promises; He is our Rock, and there is no unrighteousness in Him."[23]

- I declare an open heaven over us, in Jesus' name. Because we seek first the kingdom of God and obey Him, doors of opportunity and windows of blessing are open for us. We receive the financial favor of God. (See Matthew 6:33; Malachi 3:10.) Everyone around us can see that the Lord has granted us life and favor (see Job 10:12), and that it is He who makes all we do prosper and thrive, for the glory of God. (See Genesis 39:3–4.)

- We continually meditate on God's Word and delight in His precepts; therefore, channels of blessings run to us. We seek godly counsel and wisely choose friends; and as a result, everything we do is successful. (See Psalm 1.)

- We abound in everything good. We always have more than enough resources to spread the gospel and to help those in need. There is always abundance and never lack. (See 2 Corinthians 9:8.)

- We manage our money wisely. We are committed to paying for our dreams as we go along, so that we will not have to live with debt-driven nightmares in our future. (See Romans 13:8.)

- There is nothing lost in the economy of God. We may have made mistakes in the past, but God will restore double anything that was lost. He will turn any mistake around for our good because He is the Redeemer. (See Zechariah 9:12.)

---

23. Adapted from Psalm 92:12–15 (AMP).

- We are exceedingly blessed, and we are a blessing to others. (See Genesis 12:1–3.) Even though destruction and misfortune may be all around us, we are able to feed the hungry from our own resources. We have compassion on the depressed and beaten down; we encourage the weak and weary. As a result, our own happiness is doubled. (See Isaiah 58:10.)
- We are wise stewards. We are faithful in little things, managing every resource God has entrusted us with, so that we can rule over much, and give whenever and wherever we see a need. Because we are generous, our resources and influence multiply. (See Luke 16:10.)
- We stay alert and watchful against covetousness. We are generous, and understand that one's life does not consist of the abundance of the things we possess. (See Luke 12:15.)
- We are good providers for our families, and will leave a good inheritance, even to our children's children. (See Proverbs 13:22.)
- The Lord will guide us continually and prosper us, even in drought and famine. We will flourish like a well-watered garden. Our supply will never dry up, because God is our Source! (See Isaiah 58:11.)

Declarations of Divine Blessing, Favor, and Guidance

- I declare the perfect will of God over our lives today. I declare today that *"as for me and my house, we will serve the LORD"* (Joshua 24:15), and I ask and claim that our desires and passions are aligned with His desires and passions, and that nothing appeals to us that would not appeal to Jesus. (See Philippians 2:5.)

- We are anointed to do great things for God on a level the world is not familiar with, all for the glory of God.[24] (See Luke 4:18.)

- Circumstances are aligning themselves in our favor because we are walking in the anointing of the spirit of favor. All day long, people will go out of their way to help us because the favor of God is on us. (See Psalm 5:12.)

- We are advancing the kingdom of God. I declare new territories, new acquaintances, divine appointments, and many God-ordained relationships. (See 1 Chronicles 4:10.)

- We purposely pursue God's calling on our lives. At this very moment, He is arranging divine connections for us. We expect to meet the person or group of people who are willing to use their anointing, their power, their wealth, and their influence to connect us to our destiny. (See 1 Kings 19:19–21; Ruth 1:16.)

- We may have experienced temporary setbacks, but setbacks are only set-ups for comebacks. If life's circumstances knock us down, we will use God's wisdom, resources, strength, and perseverance to get back up again, in no time. (See Genesis 40:37–43.)

- We are overcomers. When we speak to mountains, they are removed! (See Matthew 17:20.) If the devil steals anything from us—whether health, wealth, or relationships—we demand that he repay us seven times the amount he has stolen from us! (See Proverbs 6:31.)

- We are victors. We will never have the attitude of a victim; rather, the Holy Spirit will give us creative ideas and witty inventions to deal with every situation, so that we may emerge as victors instead. (See Proverbs 8:12.)

---

24. Brim, *Life's Victories through the Anointing*.

- We are experiencing great victories, supernatural turnarounds, and miraculous breakthroughs in the midst of great impossibilities. (See Genesis 41:40.)
- We will have an incredible day today because we are too blessed to be depressed and too blessed to be stressed. We are too glad to be sad; and too anointed to be disappointed. We are too cheerful to be fearful! (See Proverbs 10:22.)

Declarations of Divine Wisdom, Knowledge, and Success

- We have wisdom far beyond our years. We are extraordinary people with incredible abilities that we will use to add value to other people's lives. We know that in helping others reach their dreams, we will reach ours, also. (See Ephesians 6:8.) We are the leaders for whom multitudes of people are looking. (See Genesis 41:39.) God has granted us wisdom and knowledge, and He will give us riches, wealth, and honor (favor) such as none has had before us, nor will anyone after us. (See 2 Chronicles 1:12.)
- We walk in discernment from the Holy Spirit, hearing His voice as He guides our lives and directs our decisions. God teaches us to profit in every endeavor. He leads us in the way we should go, so that everything we put our hands to will prosper. He gives us rain in due season and blesses all the work of our hands. (See Isaiah 48:17.)
- We are diligent to *"seek first the kingdom of God and His righteousness"* (Matthew 6:33), and then He will see to it that we always have abundance and provision. We give generously, and so we reap bountifully. (See Luke 6:38.)
- We eagerly obey God's calling on our life, and we do not procrastinate. We do not allow insecurities to delay or destroy

our assignment from God. Rather, we are ambitious and motivated, and our obedience positively affects many for the kingdom of God. (See 1 Timothy 4:14–16.)

- We will not sleep excessively, opening the door to poverty, nor will we make excuses not to work. (See Proverbs 19:15.) We are diligent, and therefore, we will eat the fruit of our labor; we will be happy, and all will go well with us. (See Psalm 128:2.)

- Our dreams come to pass through the multitude of business; we know the state of all our affairs and stay involved. We are not slothful in business, but fervent in spirit, serving the Lord. We are mindful not to waste time. (See Ecclesiastes 5:3.)

Declarations of Righteousness

- We are healthy, physically fit, and spiritually, emotionally, and intellectually equipped for our calling in Christ Jesus. (See Ephesians 4:1.) As we walk in the Spirit, the blood of Jesus cleanses us from any transgressions, and heals us from all diseases—even those trying to lurk undetected in our bodies. (See 1 John 1:7.)

- I agree with the Word of God that we are seated together with Christ in the heavenly places, far above all principalities and powers, rulers of the darkness of this age, and spiritual hosts of wickedness. We will use our delegated power in the name of Jesus to silence and nullify any attack, plan, or harassment of the enemy against us and our loved ones. (See Ephesians 2:6.)

- The grace of God is evident in our lives. We are godly role models who behave in an exemplary manner at all times. Our conduct gives no cause for criticism, but rather elicits the respect of God's people. (See 1 Timothy 4:12.)

- There is none like us on the earth. We are blameless and upright; we fear God and shun evil. Therefore, God has made a hedge around us, around our households, and around all that we have on every side. The Lord has blessed the work of our hands, and our possessions (assets) have increased in the land. (See Job 1:8–10.)
- We have made a choice to succeed today and every day hereafter. Thank You, Lord, for Your grace and power to bring my words to pass, in Jesus' name. Amen.

Declarations of Blessings Based on Deuteronomy 28

Declare these blessings over yourself, your family, and your loved ones every day. Command God's will on your lives, and watch how things will change.

Since we are faithful to obey all that the Lord our God tells us to do in His Word, He will bless and honor us. (See Deuteronomy 28:1.) All of the following blessings will settle on us since we obey Him:

- We are blessed, no matter where He assigns us to live. Our children and grandchildren are a blessing. All our labor is profitable. We have more than enough food, and plenty to give to others. No matter where we go, we are blessed. (See Deuteronomy 28: 3–5, 8.)
- The Lord will cause our enemies' plans to fail. They may start their attack, but it will completely fall apart. (See Deuteronomy 28:7.)
- The Lord will summon a blessing on our savings and investments and on all that we attempt to do. He blesses us in the homes He gives us. He blesses us with divine health. (See Deuteronomy 28:8.)

- The Lord will transform us and set us apart as His, since we do what He instructs us to do. The people around us will notice that we are special to the Lord, and they will be in awe of us. (See Deuteronomy 28:9–10.)

- The Lord will give us an abundance of prosperity—children, material goods, and productivity in our occupations and ministries. All of this will come in the place God has assigned and given us. (See Deuteronomy 28:11.)

- The Lord will open His storehouse to us so that we will have all that we need, when we need it, to do His will for our lives. He blesses all the work that we do. We will have money to lend and invest. We will never need to borrow. (See Deuteronomy 28:12.)

- We will always be on top, never at the bottom of the heap, since we obey the instructions of the Lord our God. We never swerve from them, nor will we ever make someone or something else our god. (See Deuteronomy 28:13–14.)

Scriptural Declarations of Blessings

Father, I declare and decree...

- You have been mindful of us; You will bless us. You shall increase us more and more, as well as our children and our children's children. (See Psalm 115:12, 14.)

- The work of our hands is blessed, and our possessions have increased in the land. (See Job 1:10.)

- May the Lord, the God of our fathers, make us a thousand times as many as we are and bless us as He has promised. (See Deuteronomy 1:11 AMP.)

- We are blessed (happy, and to be envied) because we believe that there will be a fulfillment of the things that were spoken to us from the Lord. (See Luke 1:45 AMP.)

Declarations to Release the Blessing into Every Part of Our Being

- Father God, I speak the blessing over our *minds* today. I declare that we have the mind of Christ and the wisdom of God flows through us. We *"let this mind be in* [us] *which was also in Christ Jesus"* (Philippians 2:5).
- Father God, I speak the blessing over our *eyes* and *ears* today. I command our eyes and ears to catch everything that is coming our way from You, Lord. (See Matthew 13:16.) We will catch Your witty inventions and creative ideas today. (See Proverbs 8:12.)
- Father God, I speak the blessing over our *hands*. Deuteronomy 28:12 says that You will bless all the work of our hands, and Psalm 1:3 states that everything we do shall prosper and come to maturity. We believe that Your Word is fulfilled in us; we have a blood covenant with You, and we are tithers and givers. (See Malachi 3:10–14.)
- Father God, I speak the blessing over our *feet*, for Deuteronomy 11:24 says that everywhere the soles of our feet shall tread will be ours, and Psalm 91:13 says we will tread upon the lion and the adder.
- Father God, I speak the blessing over our *bones* today. Proverbs 3:8 says that if we walk in humility and holiness, God will strengthen our bones. Because of the blessing, we are exempt from broken bones and from diseases of our bones. (See Psalm 34:20.)

- Father, I speak the blessing over our *bodies* today. Thank You, Jesus, that You have provided life and health to all our flesh (see Proverbs 4:22) and that You heal our wounds. (See Jeremiah 17:14.)
- Therefore, I take authority over every work of the enemy against us today, and say, "No! You will not get any pleasure out of harming us!" No weapon formed against us will be effective. (See Isaiah 54:17.) In Jesus' name, amen.

TRUST IN GOD'S FAITHFULNESS

I urge you to declare the faithfulness of God every day. Doing so is an important way to blast the devil. God's faithfulness manifests most obviously when He keeps His promises and His covenant—His Word—by fulfilling every word that goes out of His mouth. The only thing that stands to nullify His faithfulness is our own doubt and unbelief.

Especially during times of great stress and pressure, meditate on these scriptural declarations—day and night!

Scriptural Declarations of Trust in God

- *"The LORD is my rock and my fortress and my deliverer; the God of my strength, in whom I will trust; my shield and the horn [strength] of my salvation, my stronghold and my refuge; my Savior, You save me from violence. As for God, His way is perfect; the word of the LORD is proven; He is a shield to all who trust in Him. For who is God, except the LORD? And who is a rock, except our God? God is my strength and power"* (2 Samuel 22:2–3, 31–33).

- *"Some trust in chariots, and some in horses; but we will remember the name of the LORD our God"* (Psalm 20:7).

- *"For God alone my soul waits in silence; from Him comes my salvation. He only is my Rock and my Salvation, my Defense and my

Fortress, I shall not be greatly moved....My soul, wait only upon God and silently submit to Him; for my hope and expectation are from Him. He only is my Rock and my Salvation; He is my Defense and my Fortress, I shall not be moved. With God rests my salvation and my glory; He is my Rock of unyielding strength and impenetrable hardness, and my refuge is in God! Trust in, lean on, rely on, and have confidence in Him at all times, you people; pour out your hearts before Him. God is a refuge for us (a fortress and a high tower)" (Psalm 62:1–2, 5–8 AMP).

+ "For You are my hope, O Lord GOD; You are my trust from my youth [and the source my confidence!]" (Psalm 71:5).

+ The Lord is my Light and my Salvation—whom shall I fear? The Lord is the refuge and stronghold of my life—of whom shall I be afraid? When the wicked, even my enemies and my foes, come upon me to eat my flesh, they stumble and fall! For in the day of trouble He will hide me in His shelter; in the secret place of His presence will He hide me; He will set me high upon a rock—Jesus! What would have become of me if I had not believed that I would see the Lord's goodness in the land of the living? I wait and hope for and expect the Lord. I am brave and of good courage, and my heart is stout and enduring. Yes, I wait for and hope for and expect the Lord! (See Psalm 27 AMP.)

Declaration of Trust in God

The Lord is our Rock and our Fortress; our Deliverer, our High Tower; our Strength in whom we will trust. He saves us from violence; He is our Refuge and Savior. Although some trust in men and this world's system, we will remember the name(s) of the Lord our God and put our trust only in Him.

GREAT IS THY FAITHFULNESS

God has said that every generation must tell the next generation of the goodness and faithfulness of God. (See Psalm 89:1.) Use these personalized Scriptures to declare His faithfulness.

Scriptural Confessions of God's Faithfulness

- With my mouth I will make known God's faithfulness to all generations. His faithfulness has established the very heavens; even as the heavens praise Him, so shall we praise His faithfulness. O Lord God of Hosts, who is mighty like You, O Lord? Your faithfulness surrounds us; Your faithfulness and mercy go before us. Therefore, great power and prosperity are conferred upon us. You will never take Your loving-kindness from us, nor will You ever break Your covenant. You will not change any word that has gone out of Your lips. (See Psalm 89:1, 5, 8, 24, 28, 33–34 AMP.)

- Because the Lord loves us, and because He will keep the oath which He swore to our fathers, the Lord has brought us out with a Mighty Hand and redeemed us from the house of bondage, _____ (name your situation). Therefore, we know that the Lord our God, He is God, the faithful God who keeps covenant and mercy for a thousand generations with those who love Him and keep His commandments. (See Deuteronomy 7:8–9.)

- God is the Rock, His works are perfect, and all His ways are just. A faithful God who does no wrong, upright and just is He. (See Deuteronomy 32:4.)

- I know in my heart and in my soul that not one thing has failed of all the good things which the Lord our God spoke concerning us; all have come to pass for us, and not one thing has failed. (Declare this by faith, in advance!) (See Joshua 21:45; 23:14.)

- O Lord God, You are God, and Your words are true! You have promised goodness to us. (See 2 Samuel 7:28.)

- Blessed be the Lord God of Israel, who speaks to us and with His hand fulfills the Word He spoke. Lord God of Israel, there is no God in heaven above or on earth below like You, who keeps Your covenant and mercy with Your servants who walk before You with all their hearts. You have kept what You promised us; You have both spoken with Your mouth and fulfilled it with Your hand this day. (See 1 Kings 8:15, 20, 23–24, 56.)

- Blessed be the Lord God of Israel, who has fulfilled with His hands what He spoke with His mouth. The Lord has fulfilled His Word which He spoke. (See 2 Chronicles 6:4, 10.)

- The Lord is gracious to us and has compassion on us. He has respect for us because of His covenant, and He will not allow us to be destroyed; neither will He cast us from His presence. (See 2 Kings 12:23.)

- God, who has called us into fellowship with His Son, Jesus Christ our Lord, is faithful. (See 1 Corinthians 1:9.)

- The One who calls us is faithful, and He will do it. (See 1 Thessalonians 5:24.)

- But the Lord is faithful; He will strengthen and protect us from the evil one. (See 2 Thessalonians 3:3.)

- No temptation has seized us except what is common to man. And God is faithful; He will not let us be tempted beyond what we can bear. But when we are tempted, He will also provide a way out, so that we can stand up under it. (I believe this can also mean that He will not let us be tempted to be discouraged or fearful or anxious beyond what we can bear. He promises that when we are presented with an opportunity to be afraid or discouraged, He has already provided a way to escape—and that way of escape is by speaking His Word! Discipline yourself to immediately go to the Word instead of reacting to the first thing that tries to mess with your emotions). (See 1 Corinthians 10:13.)

PART III:

TOPICAL GUIDE TO BIBLICAL CONFESSIONS, DECLARATIONS, AND PRAYERS

A CHURCH OR MINISTRY

Declarations of Fruitful Ministry and Widespread Salvation

- Father God, it is not Your will that any should perish but that all should come to repentance and accept Jesus as their Savior. (See 2 Peter 3:9.) Father, I pray that Your will be done on earth as it is in heaven. (See Matthew 6:10.) I declare that _____ (name church/ministry) and _____ (name county, state, etc.) be filled with the knowledge of the glory of the Lord. (See Habakkuk 2:14.) Father, I ask that You would send laborers into the harvest fields to save lost souls. (See Luke 10:2; Matthew 9:38.)

- I declare that people will come from the north, south, east, and west. (See Luke 13:29; Psalm 107:2–3.) Every week, more and more people will come to _____. No matter where they live, or what church they attend currently, the ones who the Father wants to be here will come, and nothing will hinder them.

- These people for whom we pray are being redeemed out of the hand of the enemy right at this moment; they are becoming citizens of the kingdom of God. The lost are being saved; the backsliders are being restored; and they are being filled with the Holy Spirit. I declare that the sick, afflicted, and maimed are healed and made whole. Those who are oppressed or possessed by demons are delivered.

+ Jesus, You took the infirmities and sicknesses from those who turn to You. (See Matthew 8:17; 1 Peter 2:24.) Father, You sent Jesus, who healed us and delivered us from every destruction. Therefore, I declare all the people of this church, as well as all who visit, healed, made whole, and delivered from every sickness, disease, and infirmity, regardless of the cause or source.

+ All of these sicknesses, diseases, infirmities, and afflictions must obey the Word of the Lord and leave people's bodies now, in Jesus' name! (See Matthew 15:30–31; Psalm 107:20.) Go and do not return!

+ God is sending willing, skillful workers for every area in this ministry. The talents, abilities, ministries, and gifts of the people in this ministry are coming forth in excellence; they are being developed and used for the glory of Jesus. (See 1 Chronicles 28:21.)

+ My children and the children in this church will not be taken captive by the enemy or be his prey (see Isaiah 49:24–25); they will not give in to his temptations to sin. They are born-again, filled with the Holy Spirit, and are on fire for God. They are His children and they call Him their God. (See Jeremiah 32:38.) Their hearts are tender toward Him and they will serve, fear, and respect Him forever. (See Jeremiah 32:39.) Years later, they will train their children to do the same. (See Jeremiah 32:40.)

+ Our children hunger and thirst after righteousness and the cry of their heart is, "Come, let us go deeper into God. Let us never forget that He is our Father, and we are His children." (See Jeremiah 50:4–5.)

+ The people of this church praise and worship God in song, in dance, on instruments, and with uplifted hands. (See

Psalm 150:1–6.) They worship Him in Spirit and in truth. (See John 4:24.) They are not shy, self-conscious, or hindered by pride and religious traditions. They sing in the Spirit and with the understanding that they worship the Lord as one. (See 2 Chronicles 5:13.) His glory fills their homes and this church like a cloud. (See 2 Chronicles 5:14.)

+ The people of this church fast and pray, tearing down strongholds of the flesh. (See Matthew 17:21.) They spend time fellowshipping with God and praying in the Spirit. (See 1 Corinthians 14:4.) They are edified and built up on their most holy faith. (See Jude 1:20.)

+ The people of this church are people of the Word. They meditate on God's Word day and night (see Psalm 1:2), and they live by every Word that comes from God (see Matthew 4:4). They do not render the Word of God to no effect by the doctrines or traditions of man. (See Mark 7:13.) They do not exalt the religious beliefs of their past over the truth. They are sound in doctrine and prosper in all they do. (See Psalm 1:3.)

+ I declare that (name church/ministry) would have all the land, buildings, furnishings, equipment, supplies, and finances that are necessary to complete the work of the Father. We will have all we need, in abundance, to fulfill the works and the will of the Father. There is no lack in this church/ministry. All the people, businesses, and organizations that are represented in this body are obedient to their call to give to this church/ministry on a continual basis. (See Philippians 4:19.)

+ I ask that angels would be dispatched to go forth and create an atmosphere conducive for all these things to happen. (See Hebrews 1:13–14.) Father, may they be empowered from on high to accomplish these things. In Jesus' name, amen.

Prayer for Pastors and Ministry Leaders

Father God, I thank You that Pastor(s) _____ is/are filled with the Spirit of wisdom and revelation in the knowledge of You. (See Ephesians 1:17.) They are fulfilling Your perfect purpose and plan for their lives. They hear Your voice, and a stranger's voice they will not follow. (See John 10:27.)

I pray that the Spirit of wisdom, knowledge, counsel, might, and understanding will guide them in all of their meetings, conversations, and activities. I thank You that they'll give themselves continually to prayer and the ministry of the Word.

I thank You that they are protected from all hurt, harm, and accidents. They are the redeemed of the Jehovah God and are in covenant with Him; therefore, sickness and disease, poverty and lack, and fear and oppression have no power over them. They walk in divine health and are physically fit. Their souls prosper because they meditate in God's Word day and night. In Jesus' name, amen.

Declarations for Pastors and Ministry Leaders

- I declare that _____ (names) enjoy free time without interruption, and they are refreshed and rested for each day's work; for their youth is renewed like the eagle's. (See Psalm 103:5.)

- No weapon that is formed against them shall prosper (see Isaiah 54:17), and every lying tongue raised against them shall be silenced. Every business deal will work in their favor and advantage, and Your blessings will overtake them because they hearken diligently to the voice of the Lord their God.

- I cancel every attack of the wicked one to bring deception, distractions, hindrances, and temptations into their lives. Devil, you are bound and have no authority over our pastors, their families, or their possessions. I cover Pastor(s) _____ with the blood of Jesus; and, God, I ask that You would release Your angels to minister to them and bring them into Your best every day.
- Father, I thank You that You have opened doors for them to boldly proclaim the gospel with signs and wonders. They are teaching believers how to live independent of the world and how to have dominion over it.
- They have a clear vision, undefiled by ungodly knowledge. They are always in the right place at the right time with the right information and the right understanding. All things that are hidden in darkness are revealed to them by the light of the Holy Spirit. (See 1 Corinthians 2:10.) The anointing of increase is upon their lives; whatever they do will prosper.
- I thank You, Lord, that their families are of one heart and in one accord, and that they are enjoying heaven on the earth. Their seed is mighty upon the earth and blessed, and wealth and riches are in their house. (See Psalm 112:2–3.) They fellowship with leaders of like faith and have set a new standard of excellence for the body of Christ.

COMFORT IN TIMES OF GRIEF AND SADNESS

"Blessed are those who mourn, for they shall be comforted."
—Matthew 5:4

"Blessed be the God and Father of our Lord Jesus Christ, the Father of mercies and God of all comfort, who comforts us in all our tribulation, that we may be able to comfort those who are in any trouble, with the comfort with."
—2 Corinthians 1:3–4

"He heals the brokenhearted and binds up their wounds."
—Psalm 147:3

"Praise be to the God and Father of our Lord Jesus Christ, the Father of compassion and the God of all comfort, who comforts us in all our troubles, so that we can comfort those in any trouble with the comfort we ourselves have received from God. For just as the sufferings of Christ flow over into our lives, so also through Christ our comfort overflows."
—2 Corinthians 1:3–5 (NIV)

LOSS OF A LOVED ONE

Losing a loved one can cause such deep wounds that we wonder how we can ever recover from such a traumatic event. But, thank

God, He comes through with healing for our hearts so that we can carry on for Him and our families.

The pain of losing a loved one is staggering. But think about this: the Bible says Jesus was touched with the same feelings of our infirmities. Scripture says that we have a High Priest who understands our pain and sympathizes with us (see Hebrews 4:15); He shares in our weakness and infirmities.

When our heart is wounded to the breaking point; when we are drained of physical, mental, and emotional strength; when we are drained of the will to go on; when we have a helpless, hopeless feeling—then Jesus will come and help us, if we ask Him! He understands the feelings of our infirmities; He totally understands the "absence of strength" that we feel.

Jesus knows from personal experience our hurts, our wounds, our pains, and our feelings of having no strength to carry on. He will heal those who are broken in heart and will bind up their wounds. The key here is to draw near to Him, for when we do, He draws near to us. (See James 4:8.) We must come to Him asking for His help.

We find further instructions on dealing with grief in Hebrews 4:16, which tells us to "*fearlessly and confidently and boldly draw near to the throne of grace so that we may receive mercy and find grace to help for every need.*"

The *Amplified Bible* translates this Scripture promise as "appropriate help and well-timed help, coming just when we need it." Nothing will bring God on the scene quicker than hearing His Word spoken back to Him! Therefore, we must also speak His Word out loud and believe in our heart that the Comforter, the precious Holy Spirit, is helping us.

Pray the following prayer for yourself or someone else who is hurting.

Prayer for Comfort After Loss of Loved One

Heavenly Father, thank You that You promise comfort to those who mourn. Father, I know that You are the God of all comfort. Lord, I ask You to comfort me and fill me with Your peace. Give me the strength I need in this difficult time. I pray that You would surround me with Your love. Heal my brokenness and bind my wounds, in Jesus' name. Amen.

Scriptures to Stand On After Loss of Loved One

When Oral Roberts lost his wife, Evelyn, the Holy Spirit instructed him to memorize the following Scriptures, and I would invite you to do the same.

- Psalm 1
- Psalm 40
- Psalm 91
- Psalm 103
- Isaiah 40:31
- Romans 8:35–39
- Ephesians 6:10–20

LONELINESS

God will absolutely not forget us! He has told us Himself. *"I will not forget thee. Behold, I have graven thee upon the palms of my hands"* (Isaiah 49:15–16 KJV). The Hebrew word for *"graven"* here is *chaqaq*[25], which means "to hack" or "to engrave," as well as "to cut in stone." In other words, God "cut us in" the palms of His hands. He could have written our names in simple ink, but no! He "hacked us out" in the palms of His hands.

Remember this when you feel alone and rejected: God hacked you out on the palms of His hands. Remember this when even your best friend has turned on you: God cut you in the palms of His hands. Remember this when even that family member you counted on most has let you down: God hacked you out on the palms of His hands.

We have the following assurances, as well.

Scriptures of Assurance of God's Presence

> *Behold, I am with you and will keep (watch over you with care, take notice of) you wherever you may go, and I will bring you back to this land; for I will not leave you until I have done all of which I have told you.* (Genesis 28:15 AMP)

> *Do not fear, for I am with you; do not be dismayed, for I am your God. I will strengthen you and help you; I will uphold you with my righteous right hand.* (Isaiah 41:10 NIV)

> *God is [my] refuge and strength, a very present help in trouble.* (Psalm 46:1)

> *He satisfies the longing soul, and fills the hungry soul with goodness.* (Psalm 107:9)

> [Jesus said,] *"I am with you always, even to the end of the age."* (Matthew 28:20)

---

25. Strong's #H2710.

[Jesus said,] *"I will not leave you as orphans [comfortless, desolate, bereaved, forlorn, and helpless]; I will come [back] to you."* (John 14:18 AMP)

You are not alone; Jesus is always here. Hebrews 13:5–6 says, *"For He Himself has said, 'I will never leave you nor forsake you.' So we may boldly say: 'The Lord is my Helper; I will not fear. What can man do to me?'"*

You must, however, make the effort, and consciously make the decision that you will not allow loneliness and grief to overwhelm you. Do not get into a pity party. Instead, go to the Word of God for encouragement.

Prayer to Combat Loneliness

Father God, I ask You to fill the loneliness I am feeling with a constant reminder of how much You love me. Help me to understand that not everything in my life is over; just one part of it has ended. One season has passed, and another can now begin, with Your help, Lord.

Let this loneliness turn into compassion for other lonely people. Lead me by Your Spirit to find someone else who is lonely, and to be a friend to that person. Because I understand that I will reap what I sow, I know that You will return that friendship many times over. I come before You in the name of Jesus, asking for Your will to be done in my life. I submit my future to You, God, and purpose to please You in all I do, in Jesus' name, amen.

DEPRESSION/ DISCOURAGEMENT

If you are truly following the leading of the Holy Spirit, you will be joyful, no matter what is going on around you. Remember, you are never supposed to be "under the circumstances." You are to be *"above only, and not…beneath"* (Deuteronomy 28:13). So, confess your joy by faith, declaring, "I pass up the opportunity to be depressed, discourged, or disheartened in any way." Then proclaim the following Scripture-based declarations.

Declarations of Joy and Contentment

- I choose to bless You, Lord, at all times. I choose to praise You continually. The humble will hear my words of praise, and it will bring them joy. I join with others in magnifying You. God, we will all exalt Your name together! (See Psalm 34:1–3.)

- I put a smile on my face, knowing that Your Word says that a cheerful look can bring joy to the heart! (See Proverbs 15:30.)

- A merry heart does good like medicine, but a broken spirit dries up my bones. I will laugh today, knowing that joy is medicine and laughter is good for my health! (See Proverbs 17:22.)

- Father God, thank You for consoling me when I hurt; You give me beauty for ashes and the oil of joy when I mourn. You put a garment of praise around me and heal the spirit of heaviness. Like a tree planted right beside You, I am Your righteous child, and the healing of my heart will bring glory to You! (See Isaiah 61:3.)

- If others hate me, exclude me, revile me, and speak evil about me—for Your sake—I consider it a blessing. I actually rejoice in joy, knowing that they did the same thing to the prophets. My reward in heaven will be great! (See Luke 6:22–23.)

+ Though I may be persecuted and excluded for what I believe, I refuse to lose heart. I shake the dust off of my feet and continue walking on! My heart is still filled with joy and the Holy Spirit! (See Acts 13:50–52.)

+ You are a God of hope! You fill me with joy and peace. As I believe, I overflow in hopefulness by the power of Your Holy Spirit! (See Romans 15:13.)

+ I love righteousness and hate wickedness; and this choice to be on the side of righteousness is what anoints me with the oil of joy and lifts me so high. (See Hebrews 1:9.)

+ Though it is not always easy, I offer up a sacrifice of praise to You, God—every day and throughout my day! I acknowledge You, thank You, and confess Your holy name! (See Hebrews 13:15.)

+ I am joyful, even in times of adversity, because I know that the testing of my faith develops perseverance, and through this I am becoming mature and complete—I will lack nothing! (See James 1:2–4.)

+ I'm joyful always, I pray continually, and I give thanks in all circumstances because this is God's will for me in Christ Jesus! (See 1 Thessalonians 5:16–18.)

Declarations of Peace

Make these declarations of faith, confessing your peace in advance!

- Jesus, thank You for going to the cross for my peace, joy, and relief from grief—for taking my hurt, rejection, and sorrow. You were afflicted and smitten on my behalf. You were wounded for my transgressions, bruised for my guilt and iniquities, and this desperate need for peace was laid on Your body, too. Because of the deep wounds that were laid open on Your back, I find healing and wholeness for my body and soul! (See Isaiah 53:3–5.)

- You will guard me and keep me in perfect and constant peace as I set my mind confidently on You. (See Isaiah 26:3.)

- I am chosen and not rejected; therefore, I do not fear, because You, God, are with me. I will not be dismayed; I will accept Your strength and Your help; and You will uphold me with Your righteous hand. (See Isaiah 41:9–10.)

- Those who forget that You are the God of salvation and are not mindful that You are the Rock of all strength will reap harvests of grief and desperate sorrow—but that is not me! I know You are the God of my salvation, and I know You are the Rock of my strength! (See Isaiah 17:10–11.)

- Sorrow will not trap me. Joy always comes in the morning as I continue to speak God's Word! (See Psalm 30:5.)

- You give me strength and bless me with peace! (See Psalm 29:11.)

- Jesus, when You died on the cross, You didn't leave me without peace—You gave me Your very own peace. I will not let my heart be troubled or afraid. I will stop allowing myself to become agitated and disturbed; I will not permit myself to be fearful, intimidated, cowardly, or unsettled! (See John 14:27–28.)

- I will be anxious for nothing! In everything, by prayer and supplication and with thanksgiving, I will let my requests be made known to You—and the peace of God, which surpasses all understanding, will guard my heart and my mind through Christ Jesus! (See Philippians 4:6–7.)

EMPLOYMENT

Have you suddenly found yourself without a job? Or, do you desire a better or different job? Perhaps, you need more business and sales. First of all, be assured that God is very interested in your needs and the desires of your heart. Second, always remember that God is your Source of supply. Keep these other points in mind:

1. Give the Word of God first place in your life.

This Book of the Law shall not depart from your mouth, but you shall meditate in it day and night, that you may observe to do according to all that is written in it. For then you will make your way prosperous, and then you will have good success.

(Joshua 1:8)

2. Speak only what the Word of God says, guided by the Bible, by this book, and by other Scripture-based resources.
3. Do not let the devil steal your joy!
4. Do not quit speaking the Word and believing for its manifestation until you see it come to pass.
5. Find another believer to agree with you in prayer, and then offer up a prayer such as the one below.

Prayer for a New Job

Father, in Jesus' name, I seek Your wisdom, and trust You to direct me in seeking the job that is best for me. I will walk in mercy and truth and lean not unto my own understanding. (See Proverbs 3:3–5.) Thank You for opening wide a door for me that no man can shut (see Revelation 3:8), and thank You for giving me favor (see Psalm 5:12).

It is my desire, Father, to be debt free and to owe no man anything except to love him, as Romans 13:8 instructs me. I am willing to work diligently so that I lack nothing. (See 1 Thessalonians 4:11–12.) I know that it is Your will for me to be financially self-sufficient and for me to have an abundance to meet all of my needs, with enough left over to give generously to others. (See 2 Corinthians 9:8.)

I will not fret or have anxiety about anything, Father, for Your peace mounts guard over my heart and mind. (See Philippians 4:6–7.) Because You are my Source, I have confidence, comfort, and encouragement in Your provision. (See 2 Corinthians 1:3.) I thank You, Father, for supplying my need of employment/business, according to Your riches in glory by Christ Jesus. (See Philippians 4:19.) In Jesus' name, amen.

Confession for a New Job[26]

I released my faith for my new job on this date: _____. Therefore, by faith, I receive my new job now. I thank and praise the Lord for my new job as a _____. I see myself using the gifts and talents God has given me to _____.

---

26. Adapted from Kenneth Copeland Ministries, "My New Job Confession." http://www.kcm.org/real-help/confession/my-new-job-confession.

My faith works, and my words will come to pass. If any obstacles come my way, I will cast them aside and continue standing in faith for my new job. I know that I have been called according to God's purpose, and He works all things for good in my life, according to Romans 8:28. In Jesus' name I pray, amen.

Prayer for Favor on the Job

Father, I thank You that I have Your favor. I do not care what the situation looks like; Your favor is opening doors of opportunity. Your favor is opening doors that men say are impossible to open. Your favor is bringing abundance and success into my life. Your favor is causing people to want to help me and/or to do business with me. Your favor is causing the perfect company to hire me.

Father, I thank You that Your favor is coming on me in a new way, and it's going to turn this situation around. It's going to cause people to treat me well. I thank You that Your favor is causing potential customers to be drawn to me and to want to buy _____ from me or to hire me for my skills in doing _____. I thank You that my customers are loyal to me. My customers/employers/supervisors will give me preferential treatment because they see the blessing of God on my life.

Father, I thank You that You are causing me to be at the right place at the right time; Your favor is leading me to the right people. You are bringing wonderful financial opportunities my way. Surely goodness and mercy shall follow me all the days of my life! In Jesus' name, amen.

Declaration of Increase

Even if there is a recession in our land...

- We choose not to participate!
- We continue to sow seeds and receive this year a hundred times as much as we plant; and the Lord favors us with many blessings.
- Because of the blood that seals our covenant with Him, we become great and increase more and more, until we become very wealthy and distinguished, all for the glory of God!
- There is no recession in the kingdom of heaven!
- As we continue to seek the Lord, we will live without scarcity, and we will lack nothing.

Stand on Scripture Against Unemployment and Recession

The Scriptures below will build your confidence in the Word of God and the abundant provision that is available to believers. Memorize each one so that when the opportunity to pray and to believe God arises, the Word will already be resident in your heart.

Every time I pray for a need, I use at least one of these Scriptures. It is important that you re-speak God's Word to Him; speaking the Word out loud builds your faith, which brings the anointing and power. But it is equally important that the devil knows that you know your rights in Christ Jesus. So, get these Scriptures in your heart.

Declare these Scriptures boldly, even in the face of daunting circumstances. Refuse to be moved by what you see; believe God's Word as the final authority.

Scriptural Declarations of Prosperity

There was a famine in the land....And the Lord appeared to [Isaac] and said, Do not go down to Egypt; live in the land of which I will tell you. Dwell temporarily in this land, and I will be with you and will favor you with blessings....Then Isaac sowed seed in that land and received in the same year a hundred times as much as he had planted, and the Lord favored him with blessings. And the man became great and gained more and more until he became very wealthy and distinguished. (Genesis 26:1–3, 12–13 AMP)

God is able to make all grace (every favor and earthly blessing) come to you in abundance, so that you may always and under all circumstances and whatever the need be self-sufficient [possessing enough to require no aid or support and furnished in abundance for every good work and charitable donation]. As it is written, He [the benevolent person] scatters abroad; He gives to the poor; His deeds of justice and goodness and kindness and benevolence will go on and endure forever! And [God] Who provides seed for the sower and bread for eating will also provide and multiply your [resources for] sowing and increase the fruits of your righteousness [which manifests itself in active goodness, kindness, and charity]. Thus you will be enriched in all things and in every way, so that you can be generous, and [your generosity as it is] administered by us will bring forth thanksgiving to God.
(2 Corinthians 9:8–11 AMP)

For assuredly, I say to you, whoever says to this mountain, 'Be removed and be cast into the sea,' and does not doubt in his heart, but believes that those things he says will be done, he will have whatever he says. Therefore I say to you, whatever things you ask when you pray, believe that you receive them, and you will have them. (Mark 11:23–24)

God is not a man, that He should lie, nor a son of man, that He should repent. Has He said, and will He not do? Or has He spoken, and will He not make it good? (Numbers 23:19)

Whatever we ask we receive from Him, because we keep His commandments and do those things that are pleasing in His sight. (1 John 3:22)

Now this is the confidence that we have in Him, that if we ask anything according to His will, He hears us. And if [since!] *we know that He hears us, whatever we ask, we know that we have the petitions that we have asked of Him.*
(1 John 5:14–15)

Assuredly, I say to you, whatever you bind on earth will be bound in heaven, and whatever you loose on earth will be loosed in heaven. Again I say to you that if two of you agree on earth concerning anything that they ask, it will be done for them by My Father in heaven. (Matthew 18:18–19)

The thief does not come except to steal, and to kill, and to destroy. I [Jesus] *have come that they may have life, and that they may have it more abundantly.* (John 10:10)

Are [angels] *not all ministering spirits sent forth to minister for those who will inherit salvation?* (Hebrews 1:14)

And Jesus said to him, "Today salvation [deliverance, preservation, soundness, prosperity, rescue, joy] *has come to this house."* (Luke 19:9)

Most assuredly, I say to you, whatever you ask the Father in My name He will give you. (John 16:23)

There shall no evil befall you, nor any plague or calamity come near your tent. For He will give His angels [especial] charge over you to accompany and defend and preserve you in all your ways [of obedience and service]. (Psalm 91:10–11 AMP)

Give, and it will be given to you: good measure, pressed down, shaken together, and running over will be put into your bosom. For with the same measure that you use, it will be measured back to you. (Luke 6:38)

FAVOR

As children of God, we have a right to walk in the favor of God. Ephesians 2:7 says, "[God] *raised us up together, and made us sit together in the heavenly places in Christ Jesus, that in the ages to come He might show the exceeding riches of His grace in His kindness toward us in Christ Jesus.*"

God wants to show us something that is tangible, something you can see. *"Exceeding"* means "above and beyond." We should be experiencing His grace—His favor—in ways that are above and beyond the norm.

Some define *grace* as "unmerited favor"; however, another definition is the ability of God coming on you, enabling you to do what you cannot do for yourself! With favor, we will be able to accomplish things we have not been able to accomplish in the past.

God wants us to begin to expect Him to show up everywhere we go and in everything we do. Why? So that He can support and assist us; He wants to make things easier for us than the average person. He wants to provide us with advantages and give us special privileges.

The key to walking in this kind of favor is found in James 4:6: *"God resists the proud but gives grace to the humble."* Stay humble before the Lord and allow His favor and grace to be given to you. He loves a pure and humble heart.

TEN BENEFITS OF THE FAVOR OF GOD[27]

The favor of God...

1. Produces supernatural increase and promotion. (See Genesis 39:21.)

2. Produces restoration of everything that the enemy has stolen from us. (See Exodus 3:21.)

3. Produces honor and respect, even from our adversaries. (See Exodus 11:3.)

4. Produces increased assets, especially in the area of real estate. (See Deuteronomy 33:23.)

5. Produces great victories in the midst of great impossibilities. (See Joshua 11:20.)

6. Causes us to be recognized for our diligence and integrity, even when it seems we are least likely to be noticed. Not for our glory, but Yours, O Lord. (See 1 Samuel 16:22.)

7. Produces prominence and preferential treatment because the love of God is shed abroad in our hearts. (See Esther 2:17; Romans 5:5 KJV.)

8. Causes petitions and special requests to be granted to us, even by ungodly people. (See Esther 5:8.)

9. Causes policies, rules, regulations, and laws to be changed and reversed to our advantage. (See Esther 8:5.)

10. Causes victories in battles we won't even have to fight, for God will fight them for us! (See Psalm 44:3.)

---

[27]. Some points revised from Jerry Savelle, *Walking in Divine Favor* (Crowley, TX: Jerry Savelle Publishers, 1997).

Part III: Topical Guide to Biblical Confessions, Declarations, and Prayers 165

FAVOR WITH GOD AND MAN

No matter what you are going through, and no matter how severe it is, you are entitled to the favor of God—but you must learn to *expect* His favor. Call it in! Proclaim it! Get the angels working for you!

Confessions of Favor[28]

- Thank God that the set time of favor has come! God shall arise and have mercy upon His people. (See Psalm 102:13.)
- As God *"calls those things which do not exist as though they did"* (Romans 4:17), I call favor to show up and to surround us. The literal Greek meaning of the word for *"calls,"* kaleo, is "to summon to show up, as in a court of law."[29]
- We are the righteousness of God in Christ Jesus; therefore, we have a right to divine favor. (See 2 Corinthians 5:21.)
- The favor of God shields us from all calamity and disaster, and sickness or disease cannot live in our bodies. (See Psalm 5:12.)
- The free favor of God abounds toward us profusely! We walk in favor with God and man. (See Luke 4:19 AMP.)
- We experience preferential treatment, just as Esther, Joseph, and Daniel experienced.
- People go out of their way today to bless us, and they treat us very well, because we walk in excellence.
- I fully expect that we will be treated like those who are highly favored of the Lord, because we are!
- I expect favor to open doors of opportunity for us today—even doors that men say are impossible to open.

---

28. Some points taken from Savelle, *Walking in Divine Favor*.
29. Strong's #G2564.

- I expect God to show up in everything we do and everywhere we go!
- We associate with those who are blessed and highly favored, so that we may increase in every area of our lives.
- We operate in love; as a result, we obtain favor from God.
- We actively seek and live by God's wisdom; therefore, we are highly favored and esteemed in the sight of God and men.
- God's favor brings promotion and causes us to increase daily.
- We are blessed and highly favored of the Lord!

FEAR/WORRY

"Panic has a way of squeezing wrong words out of people's mouths. Refuse to speak anything except God's Word over the situation, and command fear and panic to leave."
—Kenneth Copeland

FEAR

Confessions of Freedom from Fear and Anxiety

- Father, in the name of Jesus, I ask You to open my eyes to any areas of fear in my life. I make the decision now and refuse to act on fear or practice it in any way. I believe that Your wisdom will flow in me, and I will be able to handle every situation that confronts me.

- From this day forward, I refuse to plant seeds of fear, and I begin a new crop of faith. I let go of fear and lay hold of life and peace. I use the words of my mouth to plant success, prosperity, love, and health by the Incorruptible Seed—the Word of God. It will prosper and grow and accomplish the purpose for which it was planted, yielding and bearing abundantly the fruits of life. I yield myself to the Spirit of Life.

- I boldly confess that the light of life in Christ Jesus is made manifest in my spirit, my soul, and my body. I believe I am firmly planted in the Lord and will flourish as a tree tended by the streams of living water. (See Psalm 1:3.) The Word of God is producing an abundant harvest in me, unhindered in any way. Therefore, I confess that I have been delivered from the fear of death. I am free from the law of sin and death. I am free from oppression, from fear, from terror; they have no place in me. I receive the peace that passes all understanding to manifest itself in my life, in Jesus' name.

- I resist all fear, in the name of Jesus. I confess I am not afraid! Even though I walk through the valley of the shadow of death, I will fear no evil! (As Jerry Savelle pointed out, the shadow of a dog never bit anyone!) I fear not, for You are with me. I am not dismayed, for You are my God. You are helping me! You are strengthening me! You are upholding me with Your right hand! You have not given me the spirit of fear, but a spirit of power, love, and a sound mind.

Confessions of Faith Rather than Fear[30]

- I have the spirit of power in me!
- I have the spirit of love in me!
- I have the spirit of a sound mind in me!
- I have the blood of the Lamb over me!
- I have the Lord going before me!
- I have Jesus within me!
- I have the angel of the Lord encamping around me!
- I have the everlasting arms of God underneath me!
- I have goodness and mercy following me all the days of my life!

30. See 2 Timothy 1:7; Hebrews 13:6; 1 John 4:18; Philippians 4:7; John 14:27–28.

♦ Thank You, Father, for the peace of God, which surpasses all understanding.

WHEN YOU ARE TEMPTED TO BE AFRAID...

Scripture to Stand On in the Face of Fear

Read aloud and meditate on this Scripture often, to keep your mind focused on God's protection, provision, and peace. Insert your name, where appropriate.

You who sit down in the High God's presence, spend the night in Shaddai's shadow, say this: "God, you're my refuge. I trust in you and I'm safe!" That's right—he rescues you from hidden traps, shields you from deadly hazards. His huge outstretched arms protect you—under them you're perfectly safe; his arms fend off all harm. Fear nothing—not wild wolves in the night, not flying arrows in the day, not disease that prowls through the darkness, not disaster that erupts at high noon. Even though others succumb all around, drop like flies right and left, no harm will even graze you. You'll stand untouched, watch it all from a distance, watch the wicked turn into corpses. Yes, because God's your refuge, the High God your very own home, evil can't get close to you, harm can't get through the door. He ordered his angels to guard you wherever you go. If you stumble, they'll catch you; their job is to keep you from falling. You'll walk unharmed among lions and snakes, and kick young lions and serpents from the path. "If you'll hold on to me for dear life," says God, "I'll get you out of any trouble. I'll give you the best of care if you'll only get to know and trust me. Call me and I'll answer, be at your side in bad times; I'll rescue you, then throw you a party. I'll give you a long life, give you a long drink of salvation!"

(Psalm 91 MSG)

Anti-Anxiety Confessions

- I come to You today, Lord, knowing that You are my God. (See Psalm 46:10.)

- By faith, Lord, I declare that I am not anxious about anything (see Philippians 4:6), for You have given me the grace to obey this command. I cast all of my anxiety upon You, knowing that You care for me. (See 1 Peter 5:7.)

- As I fix my thoughts and focus on You, Lord, You will keep me in perfect peace. (See Isaiah 26:3.)

- Your peace, O Lord, which surpasses all understanding, shall guard my heart and my mind like a fortress. (See Philippians 4:7.)

- I shall lie down in peace and sleep deeply, for You give Your beloved sleep, and their sleep is sweet. (See Psalm 4:8; 127:2; Proverbs 3:24.)

- I shall not be afraid of anything, because I speak only the Word. You, Lord, are in control and will always take care of me.

- You are faithful to provide for my every need. (See Philippians 4:19.) I shall not lack any good or necessary thing. (See Psalm 34:10.) Thank You that Your Holy Spirit is teaching me to be a good steward of all You have given me.

- No anxious thought assigned against me shall prosper, for I can take every thought captive to the obedience of Christ. (See Isaiah 54:17; 2 Corinthians 10:5.)

- I am decisive and focused, for You have given me Your Spirit of a sound and disciplined mind. (See 2 Timothy 1:7.)
- I resist addictive, obsessive, and compulsive tendencies, knowing that as I do, they must flee. (See James 4:7.)
- I will not worry about tomorrow. I live the abundant life today, trusting God to take care of tomorrow. (See Matthew 6:34.)
- I trust in You with all my heart, not relying on my own understanding, because You have ordered my steps. (See Proverbs 3:5–6.)
- You cause all things to work together for my good because I love You and have been called according to Your purpose. (See Romans 8:28.)
- I take heart and keep things in perspective, knowing that all trials last only for a season. (See James 1:2; 5:7–8.)
- Love increases and abounds in all of my relationships. (See 1 Thessalonians 3:12–13.) I can lovingly and confidently speak the truth in love, living free of bitterness and resentment. (See Ephesians 4:15; 2 Timothy 1:7.)
- I purposely bridle my tongue. I am quick to hear, slow to speak, and slow to take offense or get angry. (See James 1:19 AMP.)
- I am joyful, thankful, and positive at all times, for this is Your will for me, Father. Your joy is my strength. (See 1 Thessalonians 5:16; Nehemiah 8:10.)

Declarations for Stress Management

- I cast all my burdens and cares upon the Lord, for He cares for me; He will sustain me. (See Psalm 55:22; 1 Peter 5:7.) Yes, I will call upon the Lord in my day of distress, and He will hear and answer me. (See Psalm 18:6; 118:5.) He will redeem my soul, set me in a large place, and bring me out of all my distress. (See 1 Kings 1:29; Psalm 107:28.)

- I listen to God. I let His peace rule in my heart, and I will dwell safely, free from fear of evil. (See Colossians 3:15; Proverbs 1:33.) I do not allow my heart to be troubled or afraid, and I am anxious for nothing. (See John 14:27.) In everything, by prayer and supplication, with thanksgiving, I let my request be made known to God; and the peace of God, which passes all understanding, will keep my heart and mind through Christ Jesus. (See Philippians 4:6–7.) I remember that God will supply all my needs according to His riches in glory by Christ Jesus. (See Philippians 4:19.) He will keep me in perfect peace because I keep my mind fixed on Him. (See Isaiah 26:3.)

- I will not give up! God gives power to the faint, and to them that have no might, He increases strength. (See Isaiah 40:29.) I wait upon the Lord to renew my strength, and then I will mount up with wings as eagles; I will run and not be weary; I will walk and not faint. (See Isaiah 40:31.) I make God my Refuge and Fortress, placing all my trust in Him, and I will live in safety, preserved from trouble, surrounded by mercy, guarded by angels, sheltered from the storm, and shaded from the heat. (See Psalm 4:8; 32:7, 10; 91:11; Isaiah 25:4.)

- God is my Strength, a very present help in trouble. (See Psalm 46:1.) I call upon Him in the day of trouble, and He comes to my defense. He is my Refuge. (See Psalm 59:16.) I hide in His pavilion, set upon a Rock. (See Psalm 27:5.) I am calm in the storm, and He brings me to my desired haven. (See Psalm 107:29–30.) During troubled times, He will be with me and honor me, for His thoughts toward me are precious, and great is the sum of them. (See Psalm 139:17.) I remember that all things work together for good to those who love

God, to those who are called according to His purpose, and He will perfect that which concerns me. (See Romans 8:28; Psalm 138:8.)

- Jesus said, "Come to Me, all you who labor and are heavy laden, and I will give you rest. Take My yoke upon you and learn from Me, for I am gentle and lowly in heart, and you will find rest for your souls. For My yoke is easy and My burden is light" (Matthew 11:28–30). "Look at the birds of the air, for they neither sow nor reap nor gather into barns; yet your heavenly Father feeds them. Are you not of much more value than they? Which of you by worrying can add one cubit to his stature? So why do you worry about clothing? Consider the lilies of the field, how they grow: they neither toil nor spin; and yet I say to you that even Solomon in all his glory was not arrayed like one of these. Now if God so clothes the grass of the field, which today is, and tomorrow is thrown into the oven, will He not much more clothe you, O you of little faith?…Therefore do not worry about tomorrow, for tomorrow will worry about its own things. Sufficient for the day is its own trouble" (Matthew 6:26–30, 34).

FREEDOM FROM FEAR IN YOUR FINANCES

Declarations of Abundant Material Provision

- Father God, I thank You that as I speak Your Word concerning our finances, the angels are activated to fulfill that Word. (See Psalm 103:20.)

- We are more than conquerors through Christ Jesus, and we reign in life by Him. I say that the prince of the kingdom of

_____ (your geographical area) is defeated. I say that the principalities, powers, rulers of the darkness of this world, spirits of wickedness, seducing spirits, and devils of wrong doctrine are totally and completely defeated.

- I call their grip over our finances and material things loosed and broken. Satan and his devils are all defeated, and Jesus Christ is Lord. I speak to all of you evil spirits and command you to obey the Word of the Lord. I rebuke you and declare that your work in these things is over! (See Daniel 10:13; Ephesians 6:12; Romans 5:17, 8:37; Isaiah 54:17; 1 Timothy 4:1.)

- Father, I ask and claim that we operate in wisdom concerning our finances. We will not give heed to the lies of the enemy that would try to deceive us into buying what we should not buy, improperly using credit, and failing to tithe and give to our church and other ministries, as Your Word directs.

- We are obedient to give as the Lord directs, and the enemy's weapons of poverty and financial foolishness do not succeed in our lives.

- All our money and material things are under the lordship of Jesus. We are the Lord's faithful stewards, and we use all we have for the purpose of His kingdom.

- Exceeding abundance is multiplied to us—thousands and thousands of dollars come to us, in Jesus' name. (See 2 Corinthians 9:8.)

- Christ has redeemed us from the curse of the law—poverty, sickness, and death. (See Galatians 3:13; Deuteronomy 28.)

- For poverty, He has given us wealth; for sickness, He has given us health; for death, He has given us eternal life. (See 2 Corinthians 8:9; John 10:10.)

- We delight ourselves in the Lord, and He gives us the desires of our hearts. (See Psalm 37:4.)
- We have given, and it is being given unto us—good measure, pressed down, shaken together, and running over shall men give to us. (See Luke 6:38.)
- We have paid our tithes and given offerings; therefore, God has opened the windows of heaven and is pouring such blessings upon us that we hardly have enough room to receive them. (See Malachi 3:10.)
- We have all sufficiency in all things and abound to all good works, for our God has made all grace abound toward us. (See 2 Corinthians 9:8.)
- I speak *"great grace"* (Acts 4:33) to the mountain of lack. (In this Scripture, *"great grace"* means "operations of the power of God."[31] Speaking "great grace" to obstacles we face is an action of faith, drawing on the operations of God's great power.)
- The Lord is our Shepherd; therefore, we shall not lack any good thing. (See Psalm 23:1.) There is no lack in any area of our lives, for our God supplies all our need,s according to His riches in glory by Christ Jesus. (See Philippians 4:19.)
- The Lord has been mindful of us; He will bless us. The Lord shall increase us more and more—us and our children! (See Psalm 115:12, 14.)
- In Jesus' name, Father, I ask that You would become involved on a daily basis with Your Word that I have spoken, adding Your anointing and power to see these things accomplished. We believe that we receive the answers to our prayers.
- Father, Your Word has gone forth, and it will not return void. It will accomplish Your will and prosper as it has been sent. I have spoken according to Your will, and I believe that these

---

31. *Spirit-Filled Life Bible*, "Kingdom Dynamics," 1633.

things which I have said shall come to pass! (See Isaiah 55:11; John 14:13; Mark 11:23–24.)
- May Jesus be glorified, and You be glorified in Him, as these things are accomplished and fulfilled. In Jesus' name, by faith, we call all of these things a completed work! (See John 13:31.)
- We pass up the opportunity to be broke or in debt!

Prayer of Binding and Loosing of Finances[32]

Father God, in the name of Jesus Christ, I bind my will to the will of God, that I will constantly be aware of Your will and purpose for my life. I bind myself to the truth of God so that I will not be deceived by the many subtle deceptions of the world and the devil.

According to Matthew 18:18, I bind the strong man, so that I may spoil his household and take back every bit of material and spiritual possessions that he has stolen from me and my loved ones.

Satan, I loose your influence over every area of our finances. I loose the power of any negative words we have spoken about our financial circumstances—words such as "I'll never be able to pay my bills," "I spend everything I make," and "I'll never get out of debt." Father, forgive my words of doubt and negativity. I loose all of the wrong attitudes and patterns of thinking that I have about money, and I bind myself to the truth of Your Word, in Jesus' name. Amen.

---

32. Liberty Savard, *Shattering Your Strongholds* [revised version] (Alachua, FL: Bridge-Logos Publishers, 2001).

Scriptural Declaration of Blessings in Any Economy

Declare Psalm 112 often, even in the face of very frightening circumstances. God's Word is true. Remember, truth trumps facts every time! Remember, too, when you speak the Word, you are using your faith to speak into existence what you desire. That's the way God does it, and so should you! Do not speak what you "see"; speak what you desire, according to the Word of God.

> *Praise the Lord! (Hallelujah!) Blessed (happy, fortunate, to be envied) is the man who fears (reveres and worships) the Lord, who delights greatly in His commandments. His [spiritual] offspring shall be mighty upon earth; the generation of the upright shall be blessed. Prosperity and welfare are in his house, and his righteousness endures forever. Light arises in the darkness for the upright, gracious, compassionate, and just [who are in right standing with God]. It is well with the man who deals generously and lends, who conducts his affairs with justice. He will not be moved forever; the [uncompromisingly] righteous (the upright, in right standing with God) shall be in everlasting remembrance. He shall not be afraid of evil tidings; his heart is firmly fixed, trusting (leaning on and being confident) in the Lord. His heart is established and steady, he will not be afraid while he waits to see his desire established upon his adversaries. He has distributed freely [he has given to the poor and needy]; his righteousness (uprightness and right standing with God) endures forever; his horn shall be exalted in honor. The wicked man will see it and be grieved and angered, he will gnash his teeth and disappear [in despair]; the desire of the wicked shall perish and come to nothing.*
>
> (Psalm 112 AMP)

Prayer for Financial Breakthrough

Pray the following prayer every day to get the Word into your spirit and to renew your mind concerning your finances. Expect breakthroughs!

Heavenly Father, You say that we can come boldly before You to ask for grace and mercy in time of need. (See Hebrews 4:16.) You say that whoever asks, receives. (See Matthew 7:8; Luke 11:10.) Lord, we ask for Your wisdom to know what to do to receive a financial breakthrough.

Father, in the name of Jesus, we confess Your will over our finances today. We have given the tithe of our increase, and have given offerings, so we claim that the windows of heaven are open for us, and You are pouring out such blessings that we will not be able to contain them! Thank You for rebuking the devourer on our behalf. (See Malachi 3:10–11.)

We have given, and it is given to us, again and again and again—good measure, pressed down, shaken together, and running over. Men give into our bosom daily as we walk in love and obey Your Word. (See Luke 6:38.) Daily we have a harvest of increase. Every day, money comes to us! We increase until we are overflowing with God's abundance.

Father, You have said that You remember all our offerings and will fulfill all our petitions. (See Psalm 20:3, 5.) Thank You that You never forget a seed sown! I declare that the maximum return on our giving is ours because we give to promote the name of Jesus and the gospel in the earth.

We ask that You would teach us to prosper and to be good stewards of all that You have given us. Help us to seek Your kingdom and keep our minds fixed on You.

I declare that the God of Abraham, Isaac, and Jacob has blessed us. We are blessed, and we are a blessing to others. (See Genesis 12:1–3.) We are blessed beyond our wildest dreams and imaginations. God has empowered us to prosper to the highest degree. The glory of the Lord has risen upon us and is seen in us. (See Isaiah 60:1–2.) All who see us in our prosperity will recognize and acknowledge that we are the ones whom the Lord has blessed.

Father, Your Word says that we can decree a thing, and it will be established for us. (See Job 22:28.) This is our decree: We are out of debt, all our needs are met, and we have plenty more to put in store! We have more than enough to give into every good work! Father, I thank You for wisdom and insight to bring it to pass.

Father, we ask You for creative ideas and witty inventions that will produce a financial breakthrough. (See Proverbs 8:12.) We declare that we exercise wisdom and good judgment concerning our finances. We are filled with the knowledge of God's will in all wisdom and spiritual understanding. (See Colossians 1:9.)

We *can* know all things because we have an anointing from the Holy One! We call upon Him, and He answers us, and shows us great and mighty things (see Jeremiah 33:3)—things we need to know to prosper in every area of our lives. We declare that our minds are alert, and we hear Your voice; the voice of a stranger we will not follow. (See John 10:5.) We declare that doors of opportunity are open for our families.

God has given us power to get wealth that He may establish His covenant. We are children of covenant. We remember the Lord our God, for it is He who gives us power to get wealth. (See Deuteronomy 8:18.) Yes, it is He who has done this, for His own glory! God is the unfailing, unlimited Source of our supply. Our financial income now increases as the blessings of the Lord overtake us. (See Deuteronomy 28:2.)

The voice of the blood of Jesus Christ speaks and prophesies over our lives. The life is in the blood (see Leviticus 17:11), and the blood of Jesus speaks life and that more abundantly! The blood speaks life to the full, until it overflows!

Now, satan, we bind your activity in our lives, and we loose the angels, the ministering spirits of God, to minister to us and for us and to bring in the necessary finances, so that we may continue to finance the kingdom of God. In Jesus' name, amen.

WORRY

"Worry is nothing but meditating on the lies of the devil."
—Kenneth Copeland

Worry is "mental distress or agitation" resulting from legitimate concern over a real or imagined problem that has grown out of proportion. Worry grips us when we allow the devil to convince us that God can't—or won't, for whatever reason—help get us through this problem.

Jesus tells us not to worry about even our basic needs, because God, our heavenly Father, knows our needs and delights in providing for us. He simply wants us to give Him first place in our lives. (See Matthew 6:31–33.) We must let God have all our worries and cares for He is watching everything that concerns us. (See 1 Peter 5:7.)

Worry is a sin which must be confessed. God tells us that our worry is uncalled for; and to deny that we have sinned against Him by worrying is to fool ourselves and call God a liar. But if we confess the sin of worry, God will forgive us and cleanse us of this wrong. (See 1 John 1:8–10.)

Do not continue in this sin of faithlessness. Replace your worry with faith instead. How? By feeding on the word and thereby strengthening your faith. Remember, *"Faith comes by hearing, and hearing by the word of God"* (Romans 10:17). You must feed on the Word of God and replace those lies of the devil with the truth of God's Word. Tell satan, "I'm not thinking on your junk, in the name of Jesus. I'm thinking on the promises of God."

Worry is a habit we must break. Like any other bad habit, it must be replaced by a good habit. Remember, the definition of worry is: "Mental distress or agitation." So, in order to be freed of this habitual mental distress, you must learn, with God's help, to habitually think on good things. Study Philippians 4:8 for guidelines for right thinking, and also meditate on the following scriptural confessions.

Scriptural Confessions to Combat Worry

- I will not worry about anything; instead, I will pray about everything, telling God my needs, and I will not forget to thank Him for His answers. If I do this, I will experience God's peace, which is far more wonderful than the human mind can understand. His peace will keep my thoughts and my heart quiet and at rest, as I trust in Christ Jesus. Let me say this one more thing: I will fix my thoughts on what is true and good and right. I will think about things that are pure and lovely, and dwell on the fine, good things in others. I will think about all I am thankful for, and I will praise God. I will keep putting into practice all I have seen and learned from the great men and women of God. The God of peace is with me. (See Philippians 4:6–9.)

- God is on my side; who can be against me? Since He did not spare even His own Son for us but gave Him up for us all, won't He also surely give us everything else? (See Romans 8:31–32.)

- I give God all my worries and cares, for He is always thinking about me and watching over everything that concerns me. (See 1 Peter 5:7.)

- Worrying does no good; I trust in God. (See Joshua 1:9; Luke 12:22–34.)

- The Lord will free me from all my worries, if I will only let Him. (See Psalm 34:4.)

- Why worry? God will help me! I need only ask Him. (See Psalm 127:1–2.)

- Anxious hearts are heavy, but the Holy Spirit brings encouragement to lighten my load. (See Proverbs 12:25.)

- When I am tempted to worry, God will help me to resist that temptation. (See 1 Corinthians 10:13.)

- My problems are not the end of the world—by faith, I believe that they are the beginning of God's blessings and grace to me. (See James 1:2–5.)

- I pass up the opportunity to worry! My God is more than

God will take care of you, but you must do your part to build your faith and renew your mind using God's Word. Now, boldly say, "I pass up the opportunity to worry! My God is more than enough to meet every need I have!"

FORGIVENESS

[Jesus said,] *It is impossible that no offenses should come.*
(Luke 17:1)

It is not a question of *if* you will have the opportunity to be offended but *when*. What matters is your response. Consider the following verses:

A servant of the Lord must not quarrel but be gentle to all, able to teach, patient, in humility correcting those who are in opposition, if God perhaps will grant them repentance, so that they may know the truth, and that they may come to their senses and escape the snare of the devil, having been taken captive by him to do his will. (2 Timothy 2:24–26)

The Lord said, "Simon, Simon! Indeed, Satan has asked for you, that he may sift you as wheat." (Luke 22:31)

Jesus did not pray that Simon Peter would escape the intense shaking—He prayed that Peter's faith would not fail in the process.

Be clothed with humility, for "God resists the proud, but gives grace to the humble." (1 Peter 5:5)

Above all things have fervent love for one another, for "love will cover a multitude of sins." (1 Peter 4:8)

Tests either make you either bitter toward God and your peers, or they make you stronger.

Your spiritual maturity depends on your willingness to face, forgive, and forget past offenses. As Joyce Meyer has said, "Forgiveness is the beginning of all healing."[33]

UNFORGIVENESS IS THE DEVIL'S VICTORY

If you forgive anyone anything, I too forgive that one; and what I have forgiven, if I have forgiven anything, has been for your sakes in the presence [and with the approval] of Christ (the Messiah), to keep Satan from getting the advantage over us; for we are not ignorant of his wiles and intentions.

(2 Corinthians 2:10–11 AMP)

Notice that forgiveness is indeed the issue in these verses. Has the devil taken advantage of you? Outsmarted you? Outwitted you? Has he won a victory over you? Has he received an open door to bring more trouble into your life? If there is anybody in your life whom you are not willing to forgive, then the devil has done all these things to you!

> "FORGIVENESS IS THE BEGINNING OF ALL HEALING."
> —JOYCE MEYER

Hebrews 12:15 (NIV) says, "See to it that no one misses the grace of God and that no bitter root grows up to cause trouble and defile many." It is very important to understand that

---

33. Joyce Meyer, *Enjoying Everyday Life* broadcast.

unforgiveness, when planted in the ground of hurt, will grow a root of bitterness. Then, all sorts of ungodly things begin to grow, such as anger, hatred, manipulation, violence, and even murder! It is vital to understand also that offenses and unforgiveness are chief factors that allow the enemy to attack our health. (See Proverbs 12:4.)

Failure to forgive does us no good. What is worse, when we refuse to forgive, we expose ourselves to great harm—the devil has our number and knows where to find us! We are out from under the umbrella of God's protection and visible to the devil.

Do not let the devil outsmart you. Outsmart him instead by using the Word of God against him. Outwit him and shut the door to any further mischief from him. It's very simple: If you have anything against anyone—forgive!

Someone has said, "Unforgiveness is like drinking poison and hoping the other person dies!" Do not get caught in this trap!

Prayer of Forgiveness

Father God, I choose, as an act of my will, to forgive _____ (name) for _____ (specific offense.) Father, I ask that You would forgive him/her, as well, and not hold these charges against him/her on my account.

Father God, if there are any more negative feelings and toxic emotions buried and hidden in my soul toward _____, I ask that You would cleanse me of them. I will diligently replace these negative emotions with the fruit of Your Holy Spirit.

Father, Your Word tells us that we overcome satan by the blood of the Lamb, Jesus Christ, and the word of our testimony. I now plead the blood of Jesus over this offense and over my unforgiveness. I will not allow satan to interfere with my testimony.

Heavenly Father, I ask that You would help me regain the ground that I gave up when I held on to these offenses. I ask that You would take back this ground; I will no longer allow satan to operate there. Give me wisdom to deal with this situation in the future.

Father, I ask that You would heal now the wounded places in my soul. Heal my memory of those offenses, so that I can look back on them realistically, knowing that You have healed me.

Now, Father, I ask that You would bless _____ with Your abundant mercy. Prosper him/her in every way: body, soul, and spirit. In Jesus' name, amen.

Vikki Burke has said, "The devil will use people or situations to annoy, anger, shock, and hurt us, all with one purpose in mind: to cause us to stumble in our faith. The devil doesn't care how that is accomplished, as long as he achieves his purpose."[34] You can decide to draw close to the Lord and forgive those who have offended you, or you can pull away from them and God, put up walls, and not trust people anymore.

> UNFORGIVENESS IS LIKE DRINKING POISON AND HOPING THE OTHER PERSON DIES.

The choice really is yours, and it's as simple as making a decision to forgive. Forgiveness has nothing to do with feelings.

---

34. Vikki Burke, *Some Days You Dance* (Tulsa, OK: Word & Spirit Publishing, 2011).

WALKING IN FORGIVENESS

Once you have made a decision to forgive, pray to God, that you may walk in forgiveness.

Prayer of Commitment to Walk in Forgiveness

Father, in the name of Jesus, I make a fresh commitment to You to live in peace and harmony, not only with the other brothers and sisters of the body of Christ, but also with my family, friends, and associates.

I let go of all bitterness, resentment, envy, strife, and unkindness in any form, as an act of my will. I give no place to the devil, in Jesus' name. Now, Father, I ask Your forgiveness. By faith I receive it, having assurance that I am cleansed from all unrighteousness through Jesus Christ. I ask You to forgive and release all who have wronged and hurt me. I forgive and release them. Deal with them in Your mercy and loving-kindness.

From this moment on, I purpose to walk in love, to seek peace, to live in agreement, and to conduct myself toward others in a manner that is pleasing to You. (See Colossians 4:5.) I know that I have right standing with You and that Your ears are attentive to my prayers.

It is written in Your Word that the love of God has been poured forth into my heart by the Holy Ghost, who is given to me. (See Romans 5:5 KJV.) I believe that love flows forth into the lives of everyone I know, and that we may be filled with and abound in the fruits of righteousness, which bring glory and honor unto You, Lord, in Jesus' name. So be it! Amen.

Keep in mind that, as an act of your will, you may have to forgive over and over. When those feelings of hurt, anger, and resentment come up, emphatically resist those thoughts with the following declaration:

Declaration of Forgiveness

No! I forgave _____ on _____ (date), and I refuse to pick up that offense again. Emotions, I command you to shut up! You are not in charge; my spirit man is in charge, and I choose to forgive. You have no more power over me, in Jesus' name.

HEALTH/HEALING

"If the devil tries to put sickness on you, declare, 'Be gone, satan! That is not in my contract!'"
—Gail Winter

It is so important to regularly "declare" these healing Scriptures, even when you are well, to establish divine health. If you wait until symptoms are in your body, you will have to be even more diligent and play "catch up."

Gloria Copeland says that most people wait until they are sick to confess their healing.[35] They have it absolutely backward! Confess your healing *before* you get sick; and then, most likely, you will never get seriously ill.

When Dodie Osteen was diagnosed with a terminal disease, she saturated her spirit with biblical affirmations three times a day. She attributes her miraculous healing to her practice of consistently speaking the Word until her body eventually came into agreement with God's Word.[36]

If you are already experiencing symptoms in your body, please, stop saying how sick you are! Instead, speak these healing Scriptures. Below are some points to assist you in building your faith concerning your health and healing.

---
35. *Believer's Voice of Victory* broadcast.
36. Dodie Osteen, *Healed of Cancer* (Houston, TX: Osteen Publications, 1986).

1. Understand that the Bible is a legal covenant, sealed and ratified with Jesus' precious blood!
2. Make the Word of God the final authority in your life—not your circumstances, symptoms, or what others say.
3. Make a quality decision to believe these healing Scriptures every time you read and confess them.
4. Recite each Scripture slowly aloud so that your own ears hear the Word; for *"faith comes by hearing, and hearing by the word of God"* (Romans 10:17).
5. As I do, you may wish to use the pronouns *we* and *us* to include your loved ones.
6. Meditate on each Scripture until you receive revelation knowledge.
7. From time to time, say, *"It is written..."* (Luke 4:8; Matthew 4:10; John 10:34) before speaking a Scripture.
8. Say, "I believe that, in Jesus' name!" after every Scripture.

Scriptural Confessions of Healing

- I diligently heed the voice of the Lord my God, do what is right in His sight, give ear to His commandments, and keep all His statutes; and God will not allow any disease to come on me which is present in the world, for He is the Lord who heals me. (Say, "I believe that, in Jesus' name!") (See Exodus 15:26.)
- I walk in all the ways which the Lord my God has commanded me, and I live; it is well with me; my days are prolonged because of the inheritance which I possess in Christ. (See Deuteronomy 5:33.)
- The Lord loves me, blesses me, and multiplies me. He blesses my children and all my possessions. The Lord takes away from

me all sicknesses and will not allow any disease that is present in the world to come on me. (See Deuteronomy 7:13–15.)

- I diligently obey the voice of the Lord my God, to observe carefully all His commandments, and He sets me high above all the nations of the earth. And all these blessings shall come upon me and overtake me because I obey the voice of the Lord my God. (See Deuteronomy 28:1–14.)

- The Lord takes away from me the curse of sickness, poverty, and death. I have perfect health, for Christ has redeemed me from the curse of the law. (See Galatians 3:13.)

- The very same Spirit of God Who raised Jesus from the dead dwells in me and gives life to my mortal body through His Spirit. My faith activates that power in my body. Disease has no choice; it cannot survive in my body. The resurrection power of God drives out every trace of sickness and disease. The life of God is destroying every disease and germ in my body now. (See Romans 8:11.)

- God redeems my soul from the power of the grave, and I live eternally, for I have eternal life in Christ. (See Psalm 49:9, 15.)

- I hear God's Word and receive it, and the years of my life are many. I take a firm hold of God's Word and will not let it go, for it is my very life. (See Proverbs 4:10, 13.)

- I serve the Lord my God, and He blesses my bread and my water; He takes sickness away from the midst of me. (See Exodus 23:25.)

- God's loving-kindness is better than life. My soul shall be satisfied as with marrow and fatness, and my mouth shall praise God with joyful lips. (See Psalm 63:3, 5.)

- My soul blesses the Lord and will not forget any of His benefits, for God forgives all my iniquities and heals all my diseases.

God daily loads me with benefits. He is the God of our salvation, which includes health, welfare, deliverance, victory, and prosperity! (See Psalm 103:2–3; 68:19.)

- There is not one feeble person in my family. (Say, "I believe that, in Jesus' name!") (See Psalm 105:37.)

- God sent His Word—Jesus—and healed me; He has already delivered me from every destruction, because I have received His Word into my life. (See Psalm 107:20.)

- I choose life! I will not die (prematurely), but will live and declare the works of the Lord. (See Psalm 118:17; Deuteronomy 30:19.)

- God has saved me and healed me, and He sends prosperity to every area of my life, including my body. God revives, strengthens, and upholds me according to His Word, and I will live a long, healthy life. (See Psalm 119:25, 28, 116.)

- My heart keeps God's commandments, and length of days, long life, and peace are added to me. I fear the Lord and depart from evil. God's Word is health to my flesh and strength to my bones. When I lie down, I am not afraid. (See Proverbs 3:1–2, 7–8, 24.)

- I give attention to God's Word and consent and submit to His sayings. I do not let them depart from my eyes but keep them in the midst of my heart, for they are life to me and health to all my flesh. I aggressively guard what I think about, for my thoughts determine my attitude and my health. (Say, "I believe that, glory to God!") (See Proverbs 4:20–23.)

- I reverence and respect the Lord, and He rewards me with long life and shows me His salvation. (See Proverbs 10:27; Psalm 91:16.)

- My fruit is a tree of life, and my tongue promotes health. I walk the way of righteousness, and I have life. In my pathway there is no (premature) death. (See Proverbs 11:30; 12:18, 28.)

- My desire is only for the Lord, and it is a tree of life. I fear the Lord, and I am a fountain of life. I have a sound heart, and it is the life of my body. (See Proverbs 13:12; 14:27, 30.)

- Since life and death are in the power of the tongue, pleasant words are always in my mouth. They are as honeycomb; they are sweetness to my soul and health to my bones. (See Proverbs 16:24; 18:21.)

- I have a merry heart, and it does well, like medicine. I am satisfied from the fruit of my mouth, and from the produce of my lips I am filled. (See Proverbs 17:22; 18:20–21.)

- I follow after righteousness and mercy, and I find life, righteousness, and honor. (See Proverbs 21:21.)

- Jesus Christ has borne my grief and carried away my sorrow, my sickness, and my pain. He was stricken, smitten, and afflicted for me. He was wounded for my transgressions; He was bruised for my iniquities. The chastisement for my peace (that is, soundness and wholeness) was upon Him, and by His stripes I am healed. (See Isaiah 53:4–5; 1Peter 2:24.)

- My healing springs forth speedily, the glory of the Lord is my rear guard, and the joy of the Lord is my strength. (Say, "I believe that, in Jesus' name!") (See Isaiah 58:8; Nehemiah 8:10.)

- The Lord brings me health and healing; He heals me and reveals to me the abundance of peace and truth. (See Jeremiah 33:6.)

- Jesus took the stripes on His body for my healing; He bore my sicknesses and infirmities upon Himself while on the cross. Jesus came to destroy the works of the devil, which include sicknesses, diseases, and infirmities; therefore, all the works of the devil upon my body and mind have been destroyed. I refuse sickness and disease of every kind. I will not tolerate them; sicknesses and diseases are totally unacceptable. Jesus bore them, so I refuse to have them! I declare that I have perfect health in Jesus Christ. (See Matthew 8:17; 1 John 3:8; Acts 10:38.)

- The will of God is done on earth as it is done in heaven. There is no sickness in heaven; therefore, I will not be sick while on this earth. Jesus was never sick at all while upon this earth. Jesus is in me, and His life flows in me. As He is in the world, so am I in this world. I am healthy, even as Jesus was healthy upon this earth. (See Matthew 6:10; Galatians 2:20; 1 John 4:17.)

- All authority in heaven and earth was given to us by Jesus Christ. I have faith in the power and authority of the name of Jesus Christ, and through His name I am made perfectly well. (See Matthew 28:18; Acts 3:16.)

- I believe in God; therefore, all things are possible to me. All the promises of God are "Yes" to me, for Christ has paid the price for all of them. (See Mark 9:23; 2 Corinthians 1:19–20.)

- I have the "God kind" of faith! I speak to the mountain of sickness and disease, and it must be removed, for with God, all things are possible! (See Mark 11:22–23; Matthew 17:20; 19:26.)

- I believe that all the things which I say come to pass. All things which I desire, when I pray, I believe that I have received them, and I have them. (See Mark 11:23–24.)

- I have power and authority (that is, physical and mental strength and ability) over all the power of the enemy, including over every sickness and infirmity. Nothing shall in any way harm me! (See Luke 10:19.)

- I believe in Jesus Christ; therefore, the works that He did, I will do also. I do greater works because Jesus Christ has gone to the Father and has sent His Holy Spirit, who now lives in me. Whatever I ask in the name of Jesus, Jesus Himself does it, so that the Father may be glorified in the Son. When I ask for anything in the name of Jesus, Jesus says He will do it. (Say, "I believe that!") (See John 14:12–14.)

+ Whatever I ask of the Father in the name of Jesus Christ, He gives it to me. The Father loves Jesus Christ, and gives Him all that He asks for. The Father loves me as much as He loves Jesus, and so He gives me everything I ask. (See John 16:23, 26–27; 17:23.)

+ God's Word is the basis for my proclamation of faith; it is on my lips and in my heart. I confess with my mouth the Lord Jesus Christ and believe in my heart that God has raised Him from the dead. By faith I believe and receive righteousness, and with my mouth I declare and confirm my salvation, which includes my health and healing. (See Romans 10:8–10.)

+ I sow and reap of the Spirit eternal life. I sow words of health and healing every day, and daily reap health in my physical body. (Say, "I believe that, in Jesus' name!") (See Galatians 6:8–9.)

+ Jesus has destroyed him who has the power of death—that is, the devil. I am released from the bondage of the fear of death. Jesus has stripped satan of his authority over me; he is a defeated foe. Jesus has disarmed the demonic principalities and powers, and made a public spectacle of them, triumphing over them in the cross. (See Hebrews 2:14; Colossians 2:14–15.)

+ In the name of the Lord Jesus Christ, I have power over all demons and sicknesses, and I cast them out. Satan, you cannot touch me. I resist you, in Jesus' name. (See Mark 16:17–18.)

+ I will not be bound by the enemy. Satan cannot bind me with sickness. Healing is part of my covenant benefits, so healing belongs to me. I have a right to be released from sickness, disease, and infirmities. It is my right, and I demand that satan take his hands off me, right now! I am now loosed from any infirmity, in Jesus' name. (See Luke 13:11–13, 16.)

- My prayer and my words of faith bring healing when I am attacked with symptoms. If I have committed any sins, I am forgiven. It is all the same to God! It is as easy for God to heal me as it is to forgive my sins! (See James 5:15; Romans 10:8.)

- The Word is near me, even in my heart and in my mouth—that is, the word of faith, which I do speak! (See Deuteronomy 30:14; Romans 10:8.)

- God guards all my bones, and not one of them is broken. (Say, "I believe that, in Jesus' name!") (See Psalm 34:20.)

- It is the will of God that I should prosper and be in perfect health, even as my soul prospers. I daily renew my mind so that my soul (which includes my mind, will, and emotions) will prosper. Then I will have success and will be in good health. (See 3 John 2.)

- Jesus bore my sins upon the cross, and because of the stripes that He bore, I am healed. (See 1 Peter 2:24.)

- My body is the temple of the Holy Spirit, and all the fullness of God dwells in me. I glorify God in my body and in my spirit; my healthy body glorifies God! (See 1 Corinthians 6:19; Ephesians 1:23; 3:19.)

- No weapon formed against me shall prosper, and every tongue that accuses me in judgment, I shall condemn. This is my heritage as a servant of the Lord, for my vindication is from God, says the Lord. (Say, "I believe that, in Jesus' name!") (See Isaiah 54:17.)

- Behold, the eye of the Lord is on me because I fear Him, because I hope in His mercy. He delivers my soul from death and keeps me alive, even in famine. My soul waits for the Lord; He is my Help and my Shield. My heart shall rejoice in Him, because I have trusted in His holy name. Thank You,

Lord, that Your mercy is upon me, just as I hope in You. (See Psalm 33:18–22.)

STOP THE BLEEDING!

On a more specific note, what if you or a loved one is literally bleeding to death, whether due to a severe cut, a heavy nosebleed, a grave injury, or some other reason? Not only can you plead the blood of Jesus in the situation, but you can quote Ezekiel 16:6 and command the bleeding to stop!

The Lord said to Israel through the prophet Ezekiel, *"When I passed by you and saw you struggling in your own blood, I said to you in your blood, 'Live!' Yes, I said to you in your blood, 'Live!'"* (Ezekiel 16:6). We can speak the same words over us and our loved ones.

Declaration to Stop Bleeding

> I command the bleeding to stop *now*, and I say, "Life!" I plead the blood of Jesus, and I command you to live, in the name of Jesus!

WHEN SYMPTOMS RETURN

You can receive healing as a result of another person's faith, or from the operation of the gifts of the Holy Spirit. But, in order to maintain your healing, you must develop your own faith in God's Word concerning His healing provision. Otherwise, when the symptoms return—as surely they will—you will not be prepared to resist them.

The enemy will undoubtedly try to test your resolve to see if you truly know your covenant rights. When the devil returns with more symptoms, you will often find that they are worse than the symptoms you experienced before you prayed! You might be tempted to say, "I guess I didn't really get healed after all," or "I knew that stuff didn't work!" By saying things like this, you open the door and allow sickness to come back on you.

But if your faith is grounded in God's Word concerning healing, you can stand firm and speak the following declaration.

Declaration to Repel Recurring Symptoms

Devil, I resist you, in Jesus' name! I bind you, according to Matthew 16:19, and cancel your assignment against me. I bind the strong man, as instructed in Mark 3:27, and now I take back the healing you stole from me!

Furthermore, devil, according to Nahum 1:9, which says, *"Affliction shall not rise up the second time," Jehovah-Rapha* has already healed me, and I will not allow sickness to return.

Stand up to the devil and his cohorts! Use the name of Jesus and the Word of God to command the symptoms to leave your body. The symptoms are there illegally, so serve them an eviction notice! Hold the blood of Jesus against the enemy, and inform him that he must pass over you! (See Exodus 12:13.) The symptoms have no choice but to obey you as you speak God's Word!

THE IMPORTANCE OF COMMUNION IN HEALING

If you are going to live in divine health, there are going to be times when you will have to be downright extreme about the Word of God. There may be times when you are facing a sickness so severe that you need more than just a few moments in the Word and a quick prayer in the morning to receive your healing.

It may be time to get really serious. Consider taking Communion often—maybe even every day. The moment you wake up in the morning, before doing anything else, take Communion.

Confession in Preparation for Communion

> Lord, I dedicate my body all day today to the service of my Lord Jesus Christ. I take Jesus' pure blood shed for me.

Declaration of Healing (Communion)

> I rebuke you, satan. You are not going to put any sickness or disease on me today! Regardless of the symptoms, regardless of what my body thinks about it, by the power of Jesus, through His Spirit, I have overcome this sickness, because He who is within me is greater than he who is in the world. (See 1 John 4:4.)[37]

STEPS TO TAKE FOLLOWING COMMUNION

After taking Communion, I would thank God for my healing all day long. I would select some worship music and teaching CDs that would fill my mind and my spirit with the anointed Word of God, and I would listen to them throughout the day. In the afternoon, I would praise God and receive Communion again, to

---

[37]. Both of these prayers are from the ministry of Kenneth Copeland. http://www.kcm.org/index.php?p=daily_devotional&date=2000-09-20&devo_language=ENG&devo_choices=FTHTOFTH.

remind myself that the blood of Jesus is in my veins and that I'm part of God's family.

Concerning Communion, Jesus said, *"As often as you drink it* [the cup of My blood], *do it in remembrance of Me"* (1 Corinthians 11:25). If you are facing a serious attack of the devil, you need to remember Jesus and His shed blood all day and all night. You need to consider Jesus until thoughts of Him push the thoughts of that sickness right out of your mind!

That night before bed, I would receive Communion again, and then I would praise myself to sleep. If I woke in the night with symptoms and fear, I would open my Bible and read all the healing Scriptures, and make the devil sorry he woke me.

When the devil launches a serious attack against your body, don't mess around! Get serious about the Word. Put yourself under its constant care, and it will take care of you.

> THE ROOT CAUSE OF THE PAIN CANNOT REMAIN, IN JESUS' NAME!

HEALING PRAYER

You can build your faith on any given subject by reading what the Bible has to say about it. If you earnestly confess and meditate on the healing Scriptures, you will receive revelation knowledge that God wants you well and has already provided for your healing. Start the process by affirming your faith in prayer.

Prayer to Affirm Faith for Healing

Father, Your Word says, *"If we ask anything according to* [Your] *will,* [You hear] *us. And if we know that* [You hear] *us, whatever we ask, we know that we have the petitions that we have asked of* [You]" (1 John 5:14–15).

Father, I come to You confidently, knowing that, according to Your Word, it is Your will to heal me. It is written that the prayer of faith will save the sick, and the Lord will raise him up; and if he has committed sins, he will be forgiven. (See James 5:15–16.) I receive Your forgiveness by faith in the name of Jesus and the power of the blood of Jesus.

You said that whenever I pray, whatever things I desire, I should believe I receive them, and I shall have them, providing that if I hold anything against anyone, I will forgive that person, so that my Father in heaven may forgive me my sins. (See Mark 11:24–25.) Therefore, I let go of all unforgiveness, resentment, anger, and bad feelings toward anyone.

Your Word says in Mark 7:27 that healing is Your children's bread. I am Your child, according to Romans 10:9–10, because I have confessed Jesus as my Lord. Therefore, healing is mine. I thank You for it, Lord. Your Word says You are the Lord who heals me (see Exodus 15:26), and that by Your stripes, I am healed (see Isaiah 53:5).

Thank You, Father, for sending Your Word to heal me and to deliver me from all my destructions. (See Psalm 107:20.) Jesus, You are the Word who became flesh and dwelt among us. (See John 1:14.) You bore my griefs and pains, and carried my sorrows and sicknesses. You were pierced through for my transgressions, crushed for my iniquities; the punishment for my sins fell upon You, and because of Your stripes, I am healed. (See Isaiah 53:3–5; 1 Peter 2:24.) Therefore, I am simply not going to give in to these symptoms!

Father, I give attention to Your words and incline my ear to Your sayings. I will not let them depart from my sight but will keep them in the midst of my heart, for they are life and health to my whole body. (See Proverbs 4:20–22.) Lord, You have said that if I fear You and shun evil, this will bring health to my body and nourishment to my bones. (See Proverbs 3:7–8.) I declare that I will not die but will live and proclaim what the Lord has done. (See Psalm 118:17.) In Jesus' name, amen.

HEALING WEAPONS

Declarations of Faith for Health

- I refuse to be cast down or discouraged. Instead, I will praise You, Lord! You are the health of my countenance and my God! (See Psalm 42:11.)
- Lord my God, I thank You that I called to You for help, and You healed me! I bless You, Lord. I will not forget any of Your benefits. You forgive all my sins; You heal all my diseases. (See Psalm 30:2; 103:2–3.)
- Lord, I thank You that healing belongs to me. It is part of Your covenant with me. Father, I confess that I am a daughter/son of Abraham; therefore, I refuse to be bound by satan with any kind of sickness, disease, or infirmity. (See Luke 13:16.) Sickness is a bond of the devil, and from every bond I am loosed today!
- Jesus' blood alone qualifies me for healing and deliverance. Because of those bleeding stripes, I declare, "Devil, be gone, for it is written, *'by His stripes we are healed'*" (Isaiah 53:5).

- Devil, I resist you, in Jesus' name; I am depending entirely on the merits of Christ Jesus, by whose stripes I *was* healed. Devil, the blood of Jesus defeats you, and I resist you, because the anointing shall destroy the yoke. (See Isaiah 10:27.)

- Since the Spirit of Him who raised Jesus from the dead dwells in me, He who raised Christ from the dead will also give life to my mortal body through His Spirit, who dwells in me. (See Romans 8:11.) Thank You, Father, that I prosper and I am in good health since my soul prospers. (See 3 John 2.) I release all toxic emotions and refuse to allow them to make me sick or cause any physical manifestation.

- In the name of the Lord Jesus Christ, I exercise authority over this body of mine. Sickness and disease, I refuse to allow you to stay. This body—this house—belongs to God. It is a temple of God. I pass up the opportunity to be sick!

- Satan, you have no right to trespass on God's property. Now, get out! Leave my body! The root cause of the pain cannot remain, in Jesus' name! I have authority over you! I know it, you know it, and God knows it. I am holding fast to what I have, and I am determined to keep my healing, in Jesus' name.

> **WORDS RELEASE POWER!**

Remember, *"Death and life are in the power of the tongue"* (Proverbs 18:21). It is important not to nullify and negate your prayers by speaking words of doubt and death. Do not speak anything that disagrees with what God's Word has said about your situation. The fact may be that your body exhibits all the signs of sickness, but that is not the truth! Facts will change when subjected to the truth of the Word of God!

Declarations to Command the Body

- Body, you shut up! All symptoms lying to my body, I command you to shut up! Body, you will not be deceived! You will not listen to or obey the lies from the enemy! You are not in charge! My spirit-man is in charge. You must obey the only truth, which is the Word of God. I call divine health and healing to show up.

- Body, I demand that you come into agreement with the Word of God, which declares that by the stripes of Jesus, I was healed. Therefore, I am healed! Since I am healed, I cannot be sick! All symptoms are here illegally—they must leave *now* because the blood of Jesus bought and paid for my complete health and healing. I refuse to put up with these symptoms. The root cause of the pain cannot remain, in Jesus' name!

- Body, you listen to me; you will obey the truth, which declares that "[Jesus] *sent His word and healed them, and delivered them from their destructions*" (Psalm 107:20). Because of the stripes that Jesus bore on His back and the blood that flowed from His wounds, I am healed! I simply will not put up with these symptoms! Symptoms, be removed, right now!

Prayer to Seal Your Healing

Father God, thank You for sending forth Your healing angels today to minister complete health and healing to my body, in Jesus' name. I believe I receive, in Jesus' name, amen.

LOVE/MARRIAGE

"When we say 'I love you,' we are actually declaring, 'I will be kind to you; I will not treat you rudely, and I will not seek my own way with you. I will be longsuffering and patient with you. I will not be arrogant with you, and I will treat you with the same love and affection that Jesus gives to me. This is a definition of what it really means to love others."
—Cheryl Stegall Gipson

LOVE TALK

Prayer to Live in Love

Father, I pray that I would let no corrupt word proceed out of my mouth, but only such a word as is good for necessary edification, that it may impart grace to the hearers. (See Ephesians 4:29.)

Father, I pray that I would speak evil of no man (see Titus 3:2) and that I would restrain my lips (see Proverbs 10:19).

I pray, Lord, that I be continually filled with the Spirit, speaking to others in psalms and hymns and spiritual songs, singing and making melody in my heart to You, Lord, giving thanks always for all things to God the Father in the name of our Lord Jesus Christ. (See Ephesians 5:18–20.)

Lord, create words of faith on my lips always, since whatever I speak that is not of faith is sin. (See Isaiah 57:19; Romans 10:8; 14:23.) Father, I pray that all I speak will be spoken in love. (See 1 Corinthians 16:14.)

Jesus, I must speak words of life. Create words of life on my lips. (See Proverbs 18:21; Acts 5:20; Isaiah 57:19.) I pray that I would truly speak the very words of God. (See 1 Peter 4:11.)

Almighty God, I pray that my speech will be always in demonstration of the Spirit and of power. (See 1 Corinthians 2:4.) In Jesus' name, amen.

LOVE WALK

I encourage you to read Galatians 5 often. It will help you identify how to walk in the Spirit so that you will not fulfill the lusts (urgings) of your flesh.

Of course, you should read 1 Corinthians 13—the "love chapter"—daily if you are struggling to walk in love. Exercising the love walk will help us know how to respond in adverse situations. I encourage you to substitute the pronoun *I* for the word *love* in 1 Corinthians 13:3–8 to personalize this Scripture, and to make it your faith declaration.

Declarations of Love

- I believe nothing in my life is of any value if I do not love others! I endure long and I am patient and kind; I am not jealous or boastful or proud. I am not conceited (arrogant or inflated with pride); I am not rude and unmannerly, and I do not act unbecomingly. Because of God's love in me, I do not demand my own way or keep records of when I've been wronged. In fact, I pay no attention to a suffered wrong! I am not touchy or fretful or resentful. I do not rejoice at injustice and unrighteousness, but I rejoice whenever the truth wins out. I bear up (that is, I am emotionally stable) under anything and everything that comes. I am ever ready to believe the best of every person. I never give up, I never lose faith, and I'm always hopeful and endure patiently (with God's grace) through every circumstance. (See 1 Corinthians 13:3–8 AMP.)

+ Above all, I love others deeply and sincerely, because love covers a multitude of sins. I offer hospitality to others without grumbling. When I speak, I speak the very words of God. I serve others with the strength that God provides, so that in all things God may be praised through Jesus Christ. To Him be the glory and the power forever and ever. Amen. (See 1 Peter 4:8–9 NIV.)

Prayer of Commitment to Love

In Jesus' name, I make a fresh and strong commitment today to live the life of love, to let the tenderness of God flow through me, and to heal the wounded hearts of those I meet. Father, teach me to love, even when things go wrong; to be patient and kind always; and to overlook the spiteful words of others.

I am determined, with God's help, to make sure that all I do and say is motivated by love and by my desire to bring souls into the kingdom of our Lord Jesus Christ. I speak only the truth in love (see Ephesians 4:15), letting only such words proceed from my mouth as are good for edification, according to the need of the moment, that they may give grace to those who hear.

Father God, teach me to talk in love, to lay gossip quietly aside, and to take up words of grace instead. Lord, Your Word says that Your love is already inside me—that it has been shed abroad in my heart by the Holy Ghost and fire. (See Romans 5:5 KJV.)

So, today, I resolve to remove every obstacle that would keep that love from flowing freely in my life and into the lives of others. I put resentments behind me, and I forgive all those who have done me wrong. In the days ahead, Father, cause me to increase and excel and *overflow* with Your love. Cause me to be what this world needs most of all—a living example of Your love. In Jesus' name, amen.

MARRIAGE

Confession for a Harmonious Marriage

- Read the following Scripture aloud, substituting the names of yourself and your spouse in place of the word *"love."*

__Love__ suffers long and is kind; __love__ does not envy; __love__ does not parade itself, is not puffed up; does not behave rudely, does not seek its own, is not provoked, thinks no evil; does not rejoice in iniquity, but rejoices in the truth; bears all things, believes all things, hopes all things, endures all things.

(1 Corinthians 13:4–7)

Prayer for a Harmonious Marriage[38]

Father, in the name of Jesus, it is written in Your Word that Your love is shed abroad in our hearts by the Holy Ghost who is given to us. (See Romans 5:5 KJV.) Because You are in us, we acknowledge that love reigns supreme. We believe that love is displayed in full expression, enfolding and knitting us together in truth, making us perfect for every good work to do Your will, working in us that which is pleasing in Your sight. (See Hebrews 13:21.)

We live and conduct our marriage and ourselves honorably and becomingly. We esteem it as precious, worthy, and of great price. We commit ourselves to live in mutual harmony and accord with one another, delighting in each other, being of the same mind and united in spirit. (See Philippians 2:2.)

Father, we believe and say that we are gentle, compassionate, courteous, tenderhearted, and humble-minded. We seek peace, and it keeps our hearts in quietness and assurance. Because we follow after love and dwell in peace, our prayers are not hindered in any way, in the name of Jesus. We are heirs together of the grace of God.

Our marriage grows stronger day by day in the bond of unity because it is founded on Your Word and rooted and grounded in Your love. We decree this day that we have a marriage made in heaven! Father, we thank You for the performance of it, in Jesus' name. Amen.

---

38. Bill Winston, http://www.livingwd.org/ministries/prayerministry/confessions.

Prayer to Defeat the Spirit of Divorce

Heavenly Father, I thank You that nothing is too hard for You. All things are possible to those who believe. In the name of Jesus, I am praying and believing for reconciliation and peace in the marriage of _____. I bind the spirit of divorce. I bind pride, selfishness, and self-centeredness, and I loose the love of God.

Father, I know that nothing can change in their lives and marriage unless both _____ and _____ renew their minds according to the Word of God. Father, give them both a desire to restore their marriage, and teach them, Holy Spirit, how to change their thinking, so that it lines up with the Word of God.

I ask You, Lord, to establish peace, harmony, and unity in this marriage. I ask You to create a spirit of forgiveness. I declare that _____ and _____ are of one mind, one accord, and one flesh. I ask that You would bless this marriage and show them how to love one another. In Jesus' name, amen.

PERSONAL EDIFICATION

Declarations to Build Up Your Inner Man[39]

- Father God, this day I release words of faith into the earth—spiritual seeds that bring both a spiritual harvest and a natural, physical manifestation into our lives.

- I declare that we have no cares, for we cast the whole of our cares on Jesus, for He cares for us. We have no heavy burdens because we've taken Jesus' yoke, which is easy, and His burden, which is light. (See 1 Peter 5:7; Matthew 11:29–30.)

- I will not allow my soul to be cast down, for I put my hope and trust in God. Instead, I rejoice, knowing we are above only and not beneath; we are the head and not the tail; we are blessed coming in and blessed going out. (See Psalm 42:11; Deuteronomy 28:13.)

- We are one spirit with God, and we abide in Him always. We have the mind of Jesus Christ, and the wisdom of God flows in us and through us. Our bodies are the temple of God the Father, the Son, and the Holy Spirit. The fullness of God dwells in us—all His rule and authority—and we are complete in Him. (See Colossians 2:9; 1 Corinthians 2:16; 3:16–17; 1 Corinthians 6:19.)

---

39. Bill Winston, www.livingwd.org/ministries/prayerministry/confessions/, revised.

- We tread upon serpents and scorpions, and we exercise righteous authority over all the power of the enemy. Nothing shall by any means hurt us. (See Luke 10:19.)

- We are skilled in the Word of righteousness, and we call things that be not as though they are. We will not fear what man or evil spirits can do to us, because no weapon formed against us shall prosper. Any tongue that rises against us in judgment shall be condemned by God Himself. (See Hebrews 5:13; Romans 4:17; Isaiah 54:17.)

- The blood of the Lord Jesus Christ covers our spirits, our souls, and our bodies, and it has sanctified us and separated us from the world, the flesh, and the devil. We not only have our senses exercised to discern both good and evil, but we aggressively come against the kingdom of darkness and spoil every plot and scheme satan has waged against us and those around us. We are more than conquerors through Jesus Christ our Lord. (See 2 Corinthians 10:3–4; John 17:15–19; Romans 8:37; Hebrews 5:14.)

YOU CAN PREDICT YOUR FUTURE

You can predict your future. How? All you have to do is listen to your words. By examining the words that come out of your mouth, you will know what your future looks like—guaranteed! When you speak faith-filled declarations like the following, you can believe for a bright future filled with blessings.

Declarations to Frame Your Future

- I take my shield of faith and quench satan's every fiery dart. I declare that we will not be distracted from doing the will of God, and we will not stray to the left hand or to the right. We have sound judgment and discretion, and we refuse to be deceived by satan in any way! (See Ephesians 6:16; Proverbs 4:25–27; Psalm 89:22.)

+ We sow fruits of righteousness and will never back down from the truth. We are bold as lions, and we refuse to be intimidated by the enemy. (See Philippians 1:11; Proverbs 28:1.)

+ I declare and decree that our minds are sharp and our spirits are keenly sensitive to disturbances in the spirit realm. We watch and pray and prevent evil from taking place, because the Holy Spirit shows us things to come. We are equipped with spiritual armor and weaponry, and we are never caught off guard by the wicked one. (See John 16:13; Ephesians 6:11–18.)

+ Just as Moses' eyes were not dim or his natural vigor abated, our eyes are not dim, nor does our natural vigor decline. (See Deuteronomy 34:7.)

+ Love casts out fear, and we will aggressively love others unconditionally, for love never fails. (See 1 John 4:18; 1 Corinthians 13:8.)

+ The Lord will grant us full insight and understanding in all things. (See 2 Timothy 2:7.)

+ We are eloquent men and women, mighty in the Scriptures. We have the ability to act on the Word, and the power to accomplish whatever the Lord calls us to do. We are instructed in the way of the Lord; we are fervent in Spirit (that is, full of burning zeal) and inflamed by the Holy Spirit. We are spiritually mature. (See Acts 18:24–25.)

+ We are full of grace (that is, divine blessing and favor), and we work great signs and wonders among the people, so that no one is able to resist the intelligence, the wisdom, and the inspiration of the Holy Spirit by which we speak, because we are full of and controlled by the Holy Spirit. (See Acts 6:8.)

Declarations to Edify Your Spirit-Man

- In the name of Jesus, I am a believer. I believe God's Word. I am what the Word says I am; I have what the Word says I have; I can do what the Word says I can do.

- In Jesus' name, I render ineffective every negative word I have spoken, every negative thing I have thought—anything that has been contrary to the truth of God's Word. From this moment forward, I will acknowledge only the good things that are in me in Christ Jesus. I am saying it now: out of the good treasure of my heart, only good things will come to pass.

- We are the righteousness of God, new creations, heirs of God, and joint-heirs with Jesus. We have been delivered from the power of darkness and translated into the kingdom of God's dear Son. We have been redeemed by the blood of the Lamb—redeemed from the curse of the Law, redeemed from sickness and disease, poverty and death. (See 2 Corinthians 5:17; Galatians 3:13.)

- We can do all things through Christ who strengthens us. We are more than conquerors. He never leaves us nor forsakes us. Since the Greater One dwells with us, we can overcome every situation. The faith of God resides within us, and through it we have the victory that overcomes the world.[40] (See Philippians 4:13; Romans 8:37.)

- We are blessed (happy, and to be envied) because we believe that there will be a fulfillment of the things that were spoken to us from the Lord. (See Luke 1:45 AMP.)

---

40. http://www.lovingod.org.

- I declare, satan, that neither you nor any demonic force will rob us of God's blessings or oppress our bodies with disease or accident; nor will you destroy anything or anyone we love and hold dear, in Jesus' name! (See John 10:10.)

Declarations to Establish God's Word in Your Life

- I am the body of Christ. My body is the house of God. God lives in me, and I belong to Him. I've been bought with the price of the blood of Jesus, so I glorify God in my body, soul, and spirit. (See 1 Corinthians 6:15–20.)

- Satan has no power over me. I have been delivered from the power of darkness and translated into the kingdom of God's dear Son. Therefore, sin has no power over me. (See Colossians 1:13; Romans 6:14.)

- I submit myself to God; I resist the devil, and he flees from me. (See James 4:7.)

- I give no place or opportunity to the devil. I am careful to stay away from sin and not leave an open door for the enemy; therefore, no weapon formed against me shall prosper, and every tongue that rises against me will be shown to be wrong, and stopped! This is my heritage as a servant of the Lord; my righteousness is of Him. (See Ephesians 4:27; Isaiah 54:17.)

- Lord, You said there is no temptation that can come to me that is not common to man—nothing is beyond human resistance with the help of God. You are faithful to Your Word and to Your love for me, and You will not allow me to be tempted beyond my strength to resist. You will provide a way out, a way of escape, so I can be strong against it. (See 1 Corinthians 10:13.)

- I choose the fear of the Lord, which is to hate evil, pride, arrogance, the evil way, and the disobedient mouth. (See Proverbs 8:13.)
- I consider (that is, I fix my thoughts on) Jesus and His presence in me. (See Hebrews 12:3.)
- I love God more than anything this world offers. (See Mark 12:30.)
- I think on things that are true, honest, just, pure, lovely, and of good report. If there be any virtue or praise, I think on these things and reject all evil, worldly thoughts. (See Philippians 4:8.)
- I present my body as a living sacrifice to God—holy, devoted, and consecrated to please Him, which is a part of my spiritual worship to Him. I am not conformed to this world's way of thinking, but I am continually being transformed by the renewing of my mind to His Word, so that I can prove what is the good, the acceptable, and the perfect will of God in my life. (See Romans 12:1–2.)

Declarations to Establish Yourself in Righteousness

- Like Jesus, I love righteousness and hate iniquity. (See Hebrews 1:9.)
- I have the mind of Christ. (See 1 Corinthians 2:16.)
- I let the Word of Christ dwell in me richly in all wisdom. (See Colossians 3:16.)
- Jesus said, "*The prince of this world is coming. He has no hold on me*" (John 14:30 NIV). Just like Jesus, I decree that satan has no hold on me.

- The Holy Spirit controls my life. He produces this kind of fruit in me: love, joy, peace, patience, kindness, goodness, faithfulness, gentleness, and self-control. (See Gallatians 5:22–23.)

- I cast down imaginations and every thought that tries to exalt itself against the knowledge of God. I bring my thoughts into captivity to the obedience of Christ and His Word, having a ready mind to revenge all disobedience. (See 2 Corinthians 10:4–5.)

- In righteousness I am established. I am far from oppression. I will not fear. I am far from terror; it will not come near me. (See Isaiah 54:14.)

- I have hidden Your Word in my heart, so that I might not sin against You. (See Psalm 119:11.)

- Lord, You said if I confess and repent of my sin, You are faithful and just to forgive me of it and to cleanse me from all unrighteousness. (See 1 John 1:9.) This is the victory that causes me to overcome in this world—my faith in Jesus and in His Word. (See 1 John 5:4–5.) I live and walk by faith, not by sight or feelings. (See 2 Corinthians 5:7.)

- I live by every Word that proceeds from the mouth of God. (See Matthew 4:4.)

- The spirit of faith says, "I believe, and therefore I speak." (See 2 Corinthians 4:13.)

- I declare my desires *in advance*, and then believe that the angels and the Holy Spirit are working behind the scenes to cause God's Word to come to pass.

- I overcome the devil by the blood of the Lamb and by the word of my testimony, not loving my life so much that I am unwilling to die for Christ. (See Revelation 12:11.) The Word of God is my testimony, and by speaking it out loud and applying the blood of Jesus, I force the devil to stop his attacks.

- I shall live and not die, and I will declare the works of the Lord on this earth. (See Psalm 118:17.)
- I take heed of the ministry to which I have been called by the Lord, so that I will fulfill the work that He gave me. (See Colossians 4:17.)
- All things are working together for good in my life because I love God and I am called according to His purpose. (See Romans 8:28.)
- Thanks be to God, who gives me the victory through my Lord Jesus Christ. He always causes me to triumph. (See 1 Corinthians 15:57; 2 Corinthians 2:14.)
- Thank You, Father, that I can have all these things. I believe it in my heart. I have released it with my mouth. All will surely come to pass. (See 1 Kings 13:32.)

OVERCOME NEGATIVE CONFESSIONS

Once we are born again, we should say only the things the Word of God says. Never again should we confess anything that does not line up with God's Word.

My "Never Again" List[41]

- **NEVER AGAIN** will I confess "I can't," because the Word says, *"I can do all things through Jesus Christ who strengthens me"* (Philippians 4:13).

---

41. Adapted from Don Gossett, *What You Say Is What You Get!* (New Kensington, PA: Whitaker House, 1976), 15–16.

- **NEVER AGAIN** will I confess lack of any good thing, for *"My God shall supply all [my] need according to His riches in glory by Christ Jesus"* (Philippians 4:19)

- **NEVER AGAIN** will I confess fear, because the Word says, *"God has not given [me] a spirit of fear, but of power and of love and of a sound mind"* (2 Timothy 1:7).

- **NEVER AGAIN** will I confess doubt and a lack of faith, because the Word says, *"God has dealt to each one [every person] a measure of faith"* (Romans 12:3).

- **NEVER AGAIN** will I confess weakness, because the Word says, *"The Lord is the strength of my life"* (Psalm 27:1), and *"The people who know their God shall be strong, and carry out great exploits"* (Daniel 11:32).

- **NEVER AGAIN** will I confess that satan has any control over my life, because the Word says, *"Greater is He who is in [me] than he who is in the world"* (1 John 4:4).

- **NEVER AGAIN** will I confess defeat, because the Word says, *"God always causeth [me] to triumph in Christ"* (2 Corinthians 2:14 kjv).

- **NEVER AGAIN** will I confess a lack of wisdom, because the Word says, *"Christ Jesus…has become for [me] wisdom from God"* (1 Corinthians 1:30), and *"If any of you lacks wisdom, he should ask God, who gives generously to all without finding fault, and it will be given to him"* (James 1:5 niv).

- **NEVER AGAIN** will I confess sickness, because the Word says, *"By His stripes [I am] healed"* (Isaiah 53:5), and Jesus *"Himself took [my] infirmities and bore [my] sicknesses"* (Matthew 8:17).

- **NEVER AGAIN** will I confess bondage, because the Word says, *"Where the Spirit of the Lord is, there is liberty"*

(2 Corinthians 3:17), and *"[My] body is the temple of the Holy Spirit"* (1 Corinthians 6:19).

- **NEVER AGAIN** will I confess worries and frustration, because the Word says I am *"casting all [my] care upon Him, for He cares for [me]"* (1 Peter 5:7).

- **NEVER AGAIN** will I confess condemnation, because the Word says, *"There is therefore now no condemnation to those who are in Christ Jesus"* (Romans 8:1). I am in Christ; therefore, I am free from condemnation!

- **NEVER AGAIN** will I confess loneliness, because Jesus said, *"I am with you always, even to the end of the age [forever]"* (Matthew 28:20), and *"I will never leave you nor forsake you"* (Hebrews 13:5).

- **NEVER AGAIN** will I confess curses or bad luck, because the Word says, *"Christ has redeemed [me] from the curse of the Law, having become a curse for [me]...that the blessing of Abraham might come upon [me]"* (Galatians 3:13–14).

- **NEVER AGAIN** will I confess discontent, because the Word says, *"I have learned in whatever state [circumstances] I am, to be content"* (Philippians 4:11).

- **NEVER AGAIN** will I confess unworthiness, because the Word says, *"He made Him who knew no sin to be sin for [me], that [I] might become the righteousness of God in Him"* (2 Corinthians 5:21).

- **NEVER AGAIN** will I confess confusion, because the Word says, *"God is not the author of confusion but of peace"* (1 Corinthians 14:33), and *"Now [I] have received, not the spirit of the world, but the Spirit who is from God, that [I] might know the things that have been freely given to [me] by God"* (1 Corinthians 2:12).

- **NEVER AGAIN** will I confess persecution, because the Word says, *"If God is for [me], who can be against [me]?"* (Romans 8:31).

- **NEVER AGAIN** will I confess insecurity, because the Word says, *"When you lie down, you will not be afraid; yes, you will lie down and your sleep will be sweet. Do not be afraid of sudden terror, nor of trouble from the wicked when it comes; for the LORD will be your confidence, and will keep your foot from being caught"* (Proverbs 3:24–26).

- **NEVER AGAIN** will I confess the domination of sin over my life, because the Word says, *"The law of the Spirit of life in Christ Jesus has made me free from the law of sin and death"* (Romans 8:2).

- **NEVER AGAIN** will I confess failure, because the Word says, *"In all these things we are more than conquerors through Him who loved us"* (Romans 8:37).

- **NEVER AGAIN** will I confess frustration, because the Word says, *"You will keep him in perfect peace, whose mind is stayed on You, because he trusts in You"* (Isaiah 26:3).

- **NEVER AGAIN** will I confess fear of the future, because the Word says, *"'Eye has not seen, nor ear heard, nor have entered into the heart of man the things which God has prepared for those who love Him.' But God has revealed them to us through His Spirit"* (1 Corinthians 2:9–10).

- **NEVER AGAIN** will I confess troubles, because Jesus said in His Word, *"In the world you will have tribulation; but be of good cheer, I have overcome the world"* (John 16:33).

Positive, Faith-Filled Confessions I

Here is another outstanding teaching from Don Gossett, revised, with his permission, from his Bold Bible Missions Web site. I have shared these points with many people over the years, and they have proven to be a powerful tool in helping them change their thinking.

- I cannot talk sickness and disease and walk in health. I cannot tell others about my diseases and pains, mourning over my troubles, thereby obtaining everybody's sympathy, and still be healed. By telling others of my troubles, sorrows, pains, and aches, I invite disease and thereby nullify my right to divine health.

- Peter said, "*...casting all your cares upon Him, for He cares for you*" (1 Peter 5:7). If men on earth will extend concern to me when hearing of my difficulties, how much more will my heavenly Father show compassion to me when I am in need!

- I am learning to talk faith, and then I will be a victor in every battle. Faith-language is God's Word. I talk faith by speaking His Word. The following are examples of faith-talk: "By His stripes I am healed." "He Himself took my infirmities and bore my sicknesses." "Jesus Christ the same yesterday, today, and forever." "They shall lay hands on the sick, and they shall recover." (See Isaiah 53:4–5; Hebrews 13:8; Mark 16:18.)

- I will not have a wrong confession or a bad confession. A wrong confession is giving place to satan. I have stopped talking defeat, sickness, and weakness. Defeat is of the devil. Weakness is of the devil. Disease is of the devil. As long as I am speaking about these things, I am praising satan's works, and I can never expect to maintain victory by praising my adversary.

- My lips shall be filled with faith-words. "'The word is near you, in your mouth and in your heart' (that is, the word of faith which we preach)" (Romans 10:8). Since I am a faith-talker, I no longer moan and groan; I praise and rejoice. Faith talks cheerfully. Faith sings wholeheartedly. Faith prays believingly.

- I believe God's Word. I am bold in declaring its truth. I confess only what God says. I dare to keep that confession. I will not change it from day to day. God's Word is abiding in me, and I am abiding in it.

- I confess dominance over the devil. I believe that I'm more than a conqueror over him. In Jesus' name, I am the master of all devils. The devil knows that, and he cannot rule me any longer!

PROGRAM YOUR SPIRIT FOR SUCCESS

Make these confessions daily over you and your loved ones until the revelation truth of the Word becomes real to your spirit.

Confessions of Success

- We are the redeemed of the Lord—the people whom He has redeemed from the hand of the enemy! (See Psalm 107:2.)

- We are filled with the knowledge of God's will in all wisdom and spiritual understanding. His will is our prosperity. (See Colossians 1:9.)

- God delights in our prosperity. He gives us power to get wealth, that He may establish His covenant upon the earth. (See Deuteronomy 8:18.)

- The Lord has been mindful of us; He will bless us. The Lord shall increase us more and more, us and our children, and our children's children! (See Psalm 115:12, 14.)

- We immediately respond in faith to the guidance of the Holy Spirit within us. We are always in the right place at the right time because our steps are ordered of the Lord. (See Psalm 37:23.)

- God has given us all things that pertain to life and godliness, and we are well able to possess all that He has provided for us. (See Numbers 13:30; 2 Peter 1:3–4.)

- God is the unfailing, unlimited Source of our supply. Our financial income now increases as the blessing of the Lord overtakes us. (See Deuteronomy 28:2.)

- As we give, it is given unto us—good measure, pressed down, shaken together, and running over. (See Luke 6:38.)

- We honor the Lord with our substance and the firstfruits of our increase. Our barns are filled with plenty, and our presses burst forth with new wine. (See Proverbs 3:9–10.)

- The blessing of the Lord makes us truly rich, and He adds no sorrow with it. (See Proverbs 10:22.)

- We are like trees planted by rivers of water. We bring forth fruit in our season, our leaf shall not wither, and whatever we do will prosper. (See Psalm 1:3.)

- The grace of God even causes our mistakes prosper! (See Job 22:30.)

- We are blessed in the city, blessed in the field, blessed coming in, and blessed going out. We are blessed in the basket and blessed in the store. Our bank accounts, investments, health, and relationships flourish. The blessing of the Lord overtakes us in all areas of our lives. (See Deuteronomy 28:1–14.)

- Our God makes all grace abound toward us in every favor and earthly blessing, so that we have all sufficiency in all things, and abound to every good work. (See 2 Corinthians 9:8.)
- The Lord has opened to us His good treasure and blessed the work of our hands. He has commanded the blessing upon us in our storehouse and all that we undertake. (See Deuteronomy 28:8, 12.)
- We delight ourselves in the Lord, and He gives us the desires of our hearts. (See Psalm 37:4.)
- The Lord rebukes the devourer for our sakes, and no weapon that is formed against our finances will prosper. All obstacles and hindrances to our financial prosperity are now dissolved. (See Malachi 3:10–11; Isaiah 54:17.)
- We continually renew our mind with the Word of God; therefore, we forbid thoughts of failure and defeat to inhabit our minds. (See Ephesians 4:23.)
- We are delivered from the power and authority of darkness. We cast down reasonings and imaginations that exalt themselves against the knowledge of God, and we bring every thought into captivity to the obedience of God's Word. (See 2 Corinthians 10:3–5.)
- We are filled with the wisdom of God, and we are led to make wise and prosperous financial decisions. The Spirit of God guides us into all truth regarding our financial affairs. (See John 16:13.) The Lord causes our thoughts to become agreeable to His will, and therefore our plans are established and successful. (See Proverbs 16:3.)
- We are blessed because we choose our friends wisely and do not follow the advice of wicked people or join in with them. Blessings come to us in channels, and even during times of

Part III: Topical Guide to Biblical Confessions, Declarations, and Prayers 227

adversity, we bear good fruit. Everything we set our hands to do prospers. (See Psalm 1.)

• There is no lack in any area of our lives, for our God supplies all our needs, according to His riches in glory by Christ Jesus. (See Philippians 4:19.)

• The Lord is our Shepherd, and we do not want or lack any good thing. Jesus came so that we might have life, and that more abundantly. (See Psalm 23:1; John 10:10.)

• We live in prosperity. I say, "Peace be to us; peace to our houses, and peace to all we have!" (See 1 Samuel 25:6.)

Remember, when we give voice to God's Word on a daily basis, the angels and the Holy Spirit work diligently in arranging success in every area of our lives. They see to it that we are led by His Spirit to be in the right place at the right time, so that we will see the promises of God that we are confessing manifest in our lives and in the lives of our loved ones.

WHAT YOU CONFESS, YOU POSSESS

Remember, God used words to create. He used His Word to "frame" the worlds. (See Hebrews 11:3.) Take a moment to read Genesis 1, noting how many times you see the phrase *"God said."* In the first chapter of His Word, He used it nine times!

God doesn't do anything without saying it first. Kenneth Copeland says that that is God's MO—His method of operation.[42] If you want to be successful and walk in victory, you must use this same method of operation. You must take His words and

---

42. www.kcm.org, "Faith-to-Faith" daily devotional.

speak them out loud, until they take on form and substance and become a reality in your life.

Don Gossett of Bold Bible Missions has said, "To agree with God means to say the same thing God says in His Word about salvation, healing, answers to prayer, and everything else He tells us."[43] has graciously allowed me to share this collection of faith-filled confessions with you.

Positive, Faith-Filled Confessions II

- I confess that *"Jesus is [our] Lord"* (Romans 10:9 NIV). We possess salvation.

- I confess that *"by His stripes we are healed"* (Isaiah 53:5). We possess healing.

- I confess that the Son has made us free. (See John 8:36.) We possess absolute freedom in Him.

- I confess that *"the love of God has been poured out in our hearts by the Holy Spirit"* (Romans 5:15). We are able to share this love with others.

- I confess that we are bold as a lion. (See Proverbs 28:1.) We are bold as a lion in spiritual warfare.

- I confess that *"[He] will never leave [me] nor forsake [me]"* (Hebrews 13:5). We walk in the presence of God everywhere we go.

- I confess that we are the redeemed of the Lord. (See Psalm 107:2.) We possess redemption benefits every day!

- I confess that the anointing of the Holy One abides in us. (See 1 John 2:27.) We possess yoke-destroying power because of this anointing. (See Isaiah 10:27.)

---

43. Gossett, *What You Say Is What You Get!*, 41.

- I confess that, in the name of Jesus, we can cast out devils! (See Mark 16:17.) We possess deliverance from all devils.
- I confess that when we lay hands on the sick, they shall recover. (See Mark 16:18.) We possess healings for the oppressed!
- I confess that we are branches on the living Vine. (See John 15:5.) We possess the life of the vine in everything we do.
- I confess that we are the righteousness of God in Christ. (See 2 Corinthians 5:21.) We can stand freely in God's holy presence; we stand in satan's presence as victors!
- I confess that we are temples of the living God. (See 2 Corinthians 6:16.) God dwells in us and works through us!
- I confess that God supplies all our needs in Christ Jesus. (See Philippians 4:19.) We shall not want because we have all that we need.

CEASE ALL FOOLISH, DESTRUCTIVE TALK

If you speak words of doubt, fear, and unbelief, you may establish bad situations and circumstances in your life forever. Use the following Scriptures and prayer to negate your foolish words, and determine to speak only the Word of God over the situations in your life.

Scriptures to Cast Off Fear and Unbelief

Let the words of my mouth and the meditation of my heart be acceptable in Your sight, O LORD, my strength and my Redeemer. (Psalm 19:14)

> Search me [thoroughly], O God, and know my heart! Try me and know my thoughts! And see if there is any wicked or hurtful way in me, and lead me in the way everlasting.
> (Psalm 139:23–24 AMP)

> The entrance of Your words gives light; it gives understanding to the simple. (Psalm 119:130)

Prayer to Cast Off Fear and Unbelief

Father, in the name of Jesus, the entrance of Your Word has brought light and understanding to me. Because it is in Your Word, I believe it; from this moment forward, I will pray only my desires, as based on the Word of God. I will rebuke the problem, speak to it, and tell it to be gone!

Father, I repent of all the foolish prayers I have prayed—of all the things I have set into motion which would work against me and those I love. With the authority of my words, I break the power of every foolish word which I have spoken.

In Jesus' name, I stop every force that has been set in motion by my foolish words. I ask for Your forgiveness, and I receive that forgiveness now. I will guard my mouth and speak only that which edifies. In Jesus' name I pray, amen.

PRAYER

I admonish and urge that petitions, prayers, intercessions, and thanksgivings be offered on behalf of all men.
—1 Timothy 2:1 (AMP)

Pray at all times (on every occasion, in every season) in the Spirit, with all [manner of] prayer and entreaty. To that end keep alert and watch with strong purpose and perseverance, interceding in behalf of all the saints (God's consecrated people).
—Ephesians 6:18 (AMP)

As Christians, we are to *"pray without ceasing"* (1 Thessalonians 5:17). According to the above verses, there are different kinds of prayer. In its rendering of Ephesians 6:18, the *New International Reader's Version* urges believers to pray *"all kinds of prayers."* To get the results you desire, you must pray the correct prayer. It has nothing to do with being "legalistic" but is rather about being accurate in one's prayer life.

PRAYERS OF PETITION

The prayer of petition is one of the most effective forms of prayer when it comes to bringing about changes in your personal life—even in seemingly impossible situations. This is the prayer

> "Our prayers lay down the track on which God's power can come. Like a mighty locomotive, His power is irresistible, but it cannot reach us without rails."
> —Watchman Nee

that *changes things*, and is based on the known will of God, which is His Word, and should be written out to be most effective.

Jesus said, *"Most assuredly, I say to you, whatever you ask the Father in My name He will give you"* (John 16:23). The original Greek word that is translated as *"give"* in this passage is *didomi*,[44] meaning "to offer" or "to grant." Likewise, this verse in the *Amplified Bible* reads, *"My Father will grant you"* (AMP). The word *"grant"* reminds me of the words "funding," "gift," or "award," as used in the case of a student who receives an education grant or some other type of funding that does not need to be repaid!

As Kenneth Copeland was meditating and studying this text, he was impressed upon by the Lord to write it out and make it official, since grants are usually written in contract form. By writing it out, he would make it a point of contact for his faith. It would enable him to stay single-minded and focused on whatever he was believing of God to manifest. Then, he and his wife, Gloria, came into agreement, and they signed and dated the petition.[45]

---
44. Strong's #G1325.
45. Savelle, *In the Footsteps of a Prophet*.

The only way that you and I can truly pray in one accord is if somebody takes the time to construct a prayer by searching the Scriptures to find out what God says about the situation, and then we all pray it together.

Whenever you have a need—whether physical, spiritual, financial, or emotional—you can go to God and ask for a heavenly grant. Write out or type your petition. Use this book or a Bible concordance to help find the appropriate Scriptures. On the next page is an example of a heavenly grant or petition written in contract form. You may wish to make photocopies of it before writing on it, so that you may have a template to use for future petitions.

The prayer of petition is not an impulsive prayer but a very deliberate one—a prayer that is *on purpose*. In this prayer, you present your case before God in the form of a petition, believing that He will fulfill His promise to grant it!

There are many examples of the prayer of petition in the New Testament. To study those examples and to gain more revelation on the prayer that changes things, I encourage you to read Jerry Savelle's book *Prayer of Petition: Breaking Through the Impossible*.

Petition for a Heavenly Grant
_____

Be it known this day, _____ (date) at _____ (time), I/we receive a heavenly grant for: (list dollar amount or items, i.e., a new vehicle, salvation for my children, a new job, etc.)

_____
_____

_____

Father, in the name of Jesus, I/we come boldly to the throne of grace and present Your Word:

Jesus, You have said, "*I assure you, most solemnly I tell you, that My Father will **grant** you whatever you ask in My Name*" (John 16:23 AMP). You have also said, "*Whatever you ask for in prayer, believe (trust and be confident) that it is granted to you, and you will [get it]*" (Mark 11:24 AMP). And, Father, Your Word states, "*Give, and it will be given to you: good measure, pressed down, shaken together, and running over will be put into your bosom*" (Luke 16:38).

In accordance with Your Word, I/we give and sow _____ (dollar amount or list of nonmonetary items, such as prayer, food, good deeds, etc., which you are "planting") as seed in order to set this spiritual law to work on my/our behalf.

According to Matthew 18:18, I/we bind satan and all his forces, rendering them helpless and unable to operate. They will not hinder my/our grant from coming to pass.

According to Hebrews 1:14, I/we loose the ministering spirits, charging them to go forth and to cause my/our grant to come into my/our hands.

Jesus, You said, "*If two of you agree on earth concerning anything that they ask, it will be done for them by My Father in heaven*" (Matthew 18:19). Therefore, we set ourselves in agreement, and believe we receive now. We praise You in advance for the answer to our prayer. In Jesus' name, amen.

_____
Signature

_____
Signature

_____
Signature

_____
Signature

PRAYERS OF INTERCESSION

One of our greatest calls as Christians is to pray on behalf of others. We are called to pray without ceasing (see 1 Thessalonians 5:17) and to pray for all the saints (see Ephesians 3:18 NIV).

General Intercessory Declarations

Pray the following short declarations over your family members and friends, inserting their names and changing the pronouns as needed.

- _____ (name) prospers and is in health, even as _____'s soul prospers. (See 3 John 1:2.)
- _____ has not been given a spirit of fear, but a spirit of power and of love and of a sound mind. (See 2 Timothy 1:7.)
- _____ is not lacking in diligence but is fervent in the spirit, serving the Lord. (See Romans 12:11.)
- _____ is blessed in the city and blessed in the country. (See Deuteronomy 28:3.)
- _____ is a chosen generation, a royal priesthood, a holy nation to praise God. (See 1 Peter 2:9.)
- _____ is God's workmanship, created in Christ Jesus for good works, which God prepared beforehand, that _____ should walk in them. (See Ephesians 2:10.)

- I pray that the God of our Lord Jesus may give _____ knowledge of Him, and that the eyes of _____'s understanding will be enlightened, that _____ may know what is the hope of God's calling and what are the riches of the glory of His inheritance in the saints. (See Ephesians 1:17.)

- Pestilence and destruction will not come near _____. (See Psalm 91:6–8.)

- No weapon formed against _____ shall prosper, and every tongue that rises against _____ in judgment _____ shall condemn. (See Isaiah 54:17.)

- Though a thousand fall at _____'s side and ten thousand at _____'s right hand, no evil shall come near _____. (See Psalm 91:7.)

- _____ is blessed because _____ does not follow the advice of the ungodly; neither does _____ stand around with sinners nor join in with scoffers. _____ delights in doing everything the Lord wants. (See Psalm 1:1.)

- Wealth and riches are in _____'s house because _____ is generous and full of compassion and righteousness. (See Psalm 112:3–4.)

- _____ is full of the Holy Spirit; therefore, _____ is a powerful witness. (See Acts 1:8.)

- _____ walks in the Spirit, not fulfilling the lusts of the flesh. (See Galatians 5:16.)

- _____ shuns profane and idle babbling. _____ understands that empty chatter will lead to more ungodliness. (See 2 Timothy 2:16.)

- _____ avoids foolish and ignorant disputes, knowing that they generate strife. (See 2 Timothy 2:23.)

Part III: Topical Guide to Biblical Confessions, Declarations, and Prayers 237

- _____, a servant of the Lord, does not quarrel but is gentle, able to teach, and patient. (See 2 Timothy 2:24.)
- The fruit of the Spirit is evident in _____. Love, joy, peace, long-suffering, kindness, goodness, faithfulness, gentleness, and self-control are in strong demonstration in _____'s life. (See Galatians 5:22–23.)
- _____ is adequate and equipped for every good work. (See 2 Timothy 3:17.)
- _____ is anxious for nothing but in everything gives praise to God. (See Philippians 4:6.)
- _____ is blessed because _____ fears the Lord. Wealth and riches will be in _____'s house. (See Psalm 112:1, 3.)
- Before God formed _____ in his/her mother's womb, God knew _____ and sanctified (approved of) _____ and ordained _____ as a prophet to the nations. (See Jeremiah 1:5.)
- God called _____ by name; _____ belongs to Him. (See Isaiah 43:1.)
- _____ is the temple of God, and the Spirit dwells in _____. (See 1 Corinthians 3:16.)
- _____ will be of good courage, and God will strengthen _____'s heart as _____ waits on the Lord. (See Psalm 27:14.)
- God gives _____ the power to get wealth and establish God's kingdom. (See Deuteronomy 8:18.)
- _____ speaks the Word of God, and signs and wonders do accompany it. (See Mark 16:20.)
- _____ can do all things through Christ who strengthens _____. (See Philippians 4:13.)

- God made _____ in His image, in His likeness, to have dominion. (See Genesis 1:26.)

- I consider how I may spur _____ on toward love and good deeds. We will not give up meeting together, as some are in the habit of doing, but we will encourage one another—and all the more as we see the Day approaching. (See Hebrews 10:24–25.)

- I pray that from His glorious, unlimited resources, God will give _____ mighty inner strength through His Holy Spirit. And I pray that Christ will be more and more at home in _____'s heart as _____ trusts in Him. I pray that _____'s roots will go down deep into the soil of God's marvelous love, and that _____ will have the power to understand, as all God's people should, how wide, how long, how high, and how deep His love really is. And may _____ experience the love of Christ, though it is so great that _____ will never fully understand it. Then _____ will be filled with the fullness of life and power that comes from God. Now glory be to God! Because of His mighty power that works within _____, He is able to accomplish infinitely more than _____ would ever dare to ask or hope. May He be given glory in the church and in Christ Jesus forever and ever, through endless ages. Amen. (See Ephesians 3:16–21.)

PRAYERS FOR NATIONS AND FOR THOSE IN AUTHORITY

First Timothy 2:1–3 says that we are to pray, intercede, and give thanks for kings and all people in authority. This is God's command to every believer today. Praying for godly leaders propels us toward God's plan and purpose for our nation. The Bible says the heart of a king is in the hand of the Lord. (See Proverbs 21:1.) He can turn it however He wants, so your prayers are very important.

Prayer for Nation and Leaders[46]

Father God, in the name of Jesus, I apply the blood of Jesus over the United States of America. I hold the blood of Jesus against satan, and declare on the basis of God's Word that it overcomes every evil plot and scheme he has to destroy this country in any way.

Father, I bring the needs of our government before You and ask You to bless our nation through godly leaders. I magnify the name of Jesus and declare that He is Lord over this nation.

Father, according to 1 Timothy 2:1–3, I pray in the name of the Lord Jesus for our president, the vice president, all of the Cabinet members, and the chief justice and associate justices of the Supreme Court, to receive the wisdom of God, to act in obedience to that wisdom, and to experience the power of God flowing into their lives.

I pray for the members of the Senate and the House of Representatives, that they would find Your peace and direction, and that these men and women would act and lead according to Your Word, which says that a house divided against itself cannot stand. (See Matthew 12:25; Mark 3:25.) Therefore, I pray for them to be unified in righteousness for the sake of the nation.

I pray for Your protection to cover all of our law enforcement officers and the men and women of the military. I

---

46. Adapted from Kenneth Copeland, "A Prayer for Our Government." http://www.kcm.org/real-help/prayer/prayer-our-government.

ask for godly counsel and wisdom for judges across this land. In the name of Jesus, I pray that You and Your kingdom of righteousness would be manifested in the hearts of all those who are in authority in any way.

Declaratory Prayer for the Security of the United States

In the name of Jesus, I declare that this nation is blessed of the Lord, and no weapon formed against these United States shall prosper. (See Isaiah 54:17.)

This country is filled with people who pray and seek God's face. As a result, His eyes and ears are attuned to our prayers. (See 2 Chronicles 7:15.)

Because unseen angelic forces are working on behalf of this country, we will be victorious over our enemies. (See 2 Kings 6:16–17.)

I pray that there is no division among the citizens of this country. We form a united front by praying for our leaders daily. (See 1 Timothy 2:1–3.)

I pray that the plans for acts of terrorism are revealed to those who provide our national security. (See Daniel 11:25.)

I pray that God *"grant to us that we, being delivered from the hand of our enemies, might serve Him without fear, in holiness and righteousness before Him all the days of our life"* (Luke 1:74–75).

I am not afraid to travel, because God preserves my going out and my coming in. I carry out my daily affairs secure in the knowledge that I am more than a conqueror. (See Psalm 121:8; Romans 8:37.)

As the righteousness of God, I have authority over the enemies of the United States of America, and nothing will by any means harm us! (See Luke 10:19.)

Prayer for Jerusalem[47]

Father, Your Word says, *"Pray for the peace of Jerusalem: 'May they prosper who love you'"* (Psalm 122:6). We believe that those who love Jerusalem shall prosper, Lord Jesus; and because You love Jerusalem and wept over it, I love it, also. I pray for Jerusalem to receive the Shalom of God, which will bring wholeness to their land.

I pray that no leader of our nation will make any decision that would harm Jerusalem in any way. In the name of Jesus, I pray that You would reveal Your perfect will to all the leaders of Israel. I ask You, Lord, to reveal Yourself to each person in authority. Thank You, Father, for hearing my prayers that are in accordance to Your will.

PRAYERS OF THANKSGIVING

We should thank and praise God in advance for the answers to our prayers. And we should praise Him with our whole heart because He is good—His love for us never ends!

Prayer of Thanksgiving

I will give thanks to You, O Lord! Behold, God is our salvation! I will trust, and I will not be afraid, for the Lord God is my strength and song. (See Isaiah 12:2.) Therefore,

---

47. Adapted from Copeland, "Prayer for Our Government."

I will draw water from the wells of salvation with joy. (See Isaiah 12:3.)

Today I say, "Give thanks unto the Lord; call upon His holy name; declare and make known His deeds among the peoples of the earth; proclaim that His name is exalted!" (See Isaiah 12:4.)

I sing praises to the Lord, for He has done excellent things. (See Isaiah 12:5.) I cry aloud and shout, for great in our midst is the Holy One of Israel. (See Isaiah 12:6.)

My soul magnifies and extols the Lord, and my spirit rejoices in God my Savior! (See Luke 1:46.) For He who is almighty, *El Shaddai*, is more than enough. He has done great things for us. Holy is His name! (See Luke 1:49.) In Jesus' name, amen.

THE IMPORTANCE OF PLEASING GOD

A close and intimate relationship with God is essential to receiving answers to our prayers. When we draw close to Him, the answers will come naturally as we begin to get a revelation of His love for us.

In addition, if you are going to ask for God's help and blessings, you must seek to please Him in everything you do. It is not about works; it is about "abiding in Him." (See John 15:7.)

Make these declarations in faith.

Confessions of a Life Pleasing to God

- I always do those things that please God. (See John 8:29.) This is the motivating force of my life: to always do those things that please Him!

- Whatever I ask for, I receive of Him, because I keep His commandments and do those things that are pleasing in His sight. (See 1 John 3:22.) I acknowledge that the answers to my prayers are contingent on my doing those things that are pleasing in His sight. If my prayers are not being answered, I must seek to please Him more, and not allow an open door for the enemy. I please Him by obeying His Word and abiding in Him continually.

- Before Elijah was taken, he had this testimony, that he pleased God. (See Hebrews 11:5.) This is my heart's desire—my bold ambition—that I might have this same testimony: that I please God with my life, my time, my talents, my money, my words, my all!

- I know that without faith, it is impossible to please God. (See Hebrews 11:6.) Since I can please God only by having faith, I will boldly live the life of faith. How? By keeping the word *"near [me], in [my] mouth and in [my] heart' (that is, the word of faith which [I] preach)"* (Romans 10:8). To preach the Word, I must speak it aloud boldly. This pleases God, for *"faith comes by hearing, and hearing by the word of God"* (Romans 10:17). I am determined to speak the Word, along with hearing it, so that my faith will be strengthened.

- I do not seek to please men; for if I still pleased men, I would not be a bondservant of Christ. (See Galatians 1:10.) As a true believer, above all else, I seek to please my Lord—not with *eye* service, as men-pleasers, but as a bondservant of Christ, doing the will of God from the heart. (See Ephesians 6:6.)

- We who are strong ought to bear with the failings and the frailties of the weak and not to please ourselves, not necessarily doing what is convenient for us. Let each one of us make it a practice to make our neighbor happy, for his good and for his true welfare, to edify him, to strengthen him, and build him up, spiritually. For Christ gave no thought to His own interests. (See Romans 15:1–3 AMP.) Pleasing God means a denial of pleasing myself in order to minister to others. I strive to follow God with all my heart; I also seek to please and minister to others without compromise or fear of rejection.

- The Lord has said, *"Choose what pleases Me"* (Isaiah 56:4). Whether I eat or drink, whatever I do, I do all to the glory of God. (See 1 Corinthians 10:31.) And whatever I do, in word or deed, I do all in the name of the Lord Jesus, giving thanks to God the Father through Him. (See Colossians 3:17.) Whatever I do, I do it heartily, as to the Lord, and not to men, knowing that from the Lord I will receive the reward of the inheritance, for I serve the Lord Christ. (See Colossians 3:23–24.) I will choose to do the things that please my Lord.

- I walk worthy of the Lord, fully pleasing Him. How? By being fruitful in every good work; by being fruitful in every good work; by increasing in the knowledge of God (that is, getting to know Him better); strengthened (enabled) with all might by His glorious power, to be able to endure difficult people and situations with patience and joy; and giving thanks to the Father, who has qualified me to be a partaker of His inheritance. (See Colossians 1:10–12.)[48]

---

48. This final point was adapted from Gossett, *What You Say Is What You Get!* Revised with permission.

PROTECTION

Prayer for Protection I

Pray the following prayer often. Pray it when you've been in public; pray it after leaving work each day; pray it after ministering; pray it whenever you feel like there has been an extra onslaught of the enemy against you or any of your loved ones. Print this prayer and keep it with you at all times!

Father, in the name of Jesus, I command every spirit that is not of You, Lord, and every cohort connected to those spirits, to leave me, my family, our homes, vehicles, animals, and property, and to go to the foot of the cross, to be bound there until Jesus Christ comes back on judgment day to judge them!

I loose the holiness of God, the purity of God, and all the fruit of the Holy Spirit over myself and my loved ones.

Lord, cover us with the blood of Jesus from the top of our heads to the soles of our feet—our spirit, soul (our mind, will, and emotions), and body—so that no weapon formed against us shall prosper, and every tongue that rises against us in judgment will be shown to be in the wrong. (See Isaiah 54:17.) And, Lord, I thank You for covering us and all our possessions with the precious blood of Jesus Christ, in whose name I pray, amen![49]

Prayer for Protection II

Heavenly Father, please guard us as the apple of Your eye. Hide us in the shadow of Your wings. Protect us from wicked people and evil spirits who try to attack us, and from murderous enemies who surround us. (See Psalm 17:8–9.)

Father God, we receive You as our Protection and our Covering. We are Your children by the blood of Jesus. Your blood covers, sanctifies, cleanses, and protects us and our loved ones. We depend on it!

As our Protector, You give Your angels charge over us in all our ways. They hold us up in their hands to keep our feet from stumbling. With long life You satisfy us and show us Your salvation. (See Psalm 91:11–16.)

We will not be afraid, for You are with us, and You will never leave us nor forsake us. No weapon that is formed against us will be successful. This is our heritage because our righteousness is of You. (See Hebrews 13:5; Isaiah 54:17.)

Thank You, Father, for Your love, Your gentleness, Your forgiveness, and Your protection. I know that it is not Your will for anything bad to happen to us or our loved ones. Therefore, I boldly proclaim that You are our Fortress, our God, and our Refuge; we trust in You! (See Psalm 91:2.)

---

49. Janice Smith is a personal friend and an ordained minister. She is the one who taught me this prayer and the importance of praying it.

Because You are for us, who can be against us? Because You love us, nothing can separate us from that love—not hate, persecution, lying, gossip, slander, criticism, or even death. No evil shall befall us, nor shall any plague of any kind come near any of us, in Jesus' name. Your Word is our armor and protection, and we shall not be afraid of the terror at night, or of the arrow that flies by day, or the pestilence that walks in darkness. (See Romans 8:38–39; Psalm 91:5.)

Thank You, Father, that You love us and care for us today. We are fully under Your protection! Thank You for the blood of Jesus. The enemy must pass over us! (See Exodus 12:13.)

We pray these things in the name of Jesus, amen.

THE ARMOR OF GOD

Putting on the armor of God (see Ephesians 6:10–18) is simply making a conscious decision to "put on" the attributes of Jesus Himself—which are truth, righteousness, peace, faith, salvation, and so on. When we demonstrate these characteristics, we leave no open door for the enemy; therefore, we are able to stand firm against the schemes of the devil. Dressing ourselves in the whole armor of God is literally putting on the Lord Jesus Christ, so that we are protected and preserved from harm.

Prayer for Putting On the Armor of God

Father God, in Jesus' name, according to Ephesians 6:10–18, I put on...

- The belt of truth. (See Ephesians 6:14.) I will fill my innermost parts with Your Word, for *"Your word is truth"* (John 17:17). I determine to walk in truth and not be deceived by the enemy.

- The breastplate of righteousness. (See Ephesians 6:14.) I will walk in Your righteousness, Lord, covered by the blood of Jesus. I allow His righteousness to influence my mind and transform me into the image of God.

- The shoes of the gospel of peace. (See Ephesians 6:15.) I will walk in the peace of God, which gives me the stability and readiness to proclaim the gospel to those in my path today.

- I lift up the shield of faith. (See Ephesians 6:16.) I will exercise my faith by speaking Your Word in every situation. Armed with the Word of God, we can withstand the attacks of the enemy and render his fiery darts ineffective.

- The helmet of salvation. (See Ephesians 6:17.) I will speak Your Word, which will shelter my mind from satan's attacks of doubt, discouragement, and temptation.

- The sword of the Spirit. (See Ephesians 6:17.) I wield the sword of the Spirit, which is praying the Word of God—I use Your Word as a sword to defeat the devil. Just as Jesus did in the wilderness, I declare, *"It is written…"* (Matthew 4:4, 6, 7, 10; Luke 4:4, 8, 10) to every circumstance and situation that confronts us.

- Continual prayer. (See Ephesians 6:18.) I pray in the Spirit at all times and in every situation. This causes me to persevere and be alert.

- The garment of praise. (See Isaiah 61:3.) I put on the garment of praise and resist the spirit of heaviness. I have made a decision to praise You, Lord, in all things today, no matter what.

Now, Father God, I place each piece of Your armor on _____ (names), declaring by faith that they also stand firm against the schemes of the devil. In Jesus' name, amen.

Declaration of Protection Based on Psalm 91

I declare with total trust and confidence that…

- We are dwelling in the secret place of the Most High!
- We are abiding under the shadow of the Almighty!
- You, God, are our Fortress! You are our Refuge!
- In You, God, we put our trust!
- You deliver us from those who try to trap us!
- You hide us from the enemy with Your feathers!
- We will not live in fear!
- We are inaccessible to the enemy in the secret place!
- No evil, *no* calamity, *no* sickness or disease will come near us!
- The angels are watching over us and keeping us safe in all our ways, because we have known Your ways, O Lord!
- You are delivering us from trouble!
- You are our Salvation!

SALVATION AND SPIRITUAL GROWTH

SALVATION

Each of the Scriptures below is a salvation promise. When they are proclaimed to the heart of an unbeliever, it imparts faith that enables the unsaved to believe and receive God's blessed promise of salvation. When this happens, a marvelous miracle of personal transformation takes place.

Scriptures of Salvation

As many as received Him, to them He gave the right to become children of God, to those who believe in His name. (John 1:12)

For God so loved the world that He gave His only begotten Son, that whoever believes in Him should not perish but have everlasting life. (John 3:16)

Therefore, if anyone is in Christ, he is a new creation; old things have passed away; behold, all things have become new. (2 Corinthians 5:17)

For by grace you have been saved through faith, and that not of yourselves; it is the gift of God, not of works, lest anyone should boast. (Ephesians 2:8–9)

If you confess with your mouth the Lord Jesus and believe in your heart that God has raised Him from the dead, you will be saved. For with the heart one believes unto righteousness, and with the mouth confession is made unto salvation.

(Romans 10:9–10)

Personal Salvation Prayer

If you truly believe that Jesus is the Son of God, that He was crucified on a cross, buried, and raised from the dead, then pray this prayer to be born again:

> Dear heavenly Father, I thank You for loving me and for sending Your Son Jesus to redeem me. I believe in my heart, and now confess with my lips, that Jesus Christ is God Himself, come to this earth to save me. I believe that Jesus died on the cross for my sins and was buried; He rose again on the third day and is alive at the right hand of God today.
>
> Dear Jesus, I ask You to come into my heart and forgive me of my sins, as I repent of them now. I proclaim You as my Savior and Lord. From this moment forward, with Your help, I will live for You. Amen.

SALVATION FOR OTHERS

God is very interested in the salvation of our loved ones—especially our family members.; He knows how much we love and care about them, and so His promises always include everyone in our family unit. The influence of only one in a household initially believing is significant, as proven by the following examples from the Bible:

- Noah prepared the ark for *"the saving of his household"* (Hebrews 11:7).
- God sent Joseph to Egypt for the ultimate salvation of his entire family. (See Genesis 45:7, 18; 50:20.)
- Moses took a *"lamb for each household"* (Exodus 12:3) to sacrifice during Passover.
- Rahab asked for the saving of her house, which would have included the family's servants. (See Joshua 2:12–14.)
- Cornelius called together his relatives and close friends, all of whom were saved and filled with the Holy Spirit. (See Acts 10.)

Scriptural Assurances of Salvation for Family Members

There are biblical promises of salvation that apply specifically to your family:

- *"Believe in the Lord Jesus, and you will be saved,* **you and your household***"* (Acts 16:31). Believe that your entire household will be saved simply because you are saved. Even if they no longer live under your roof, they are still a part of your household.
- *"Today salvation has come to* **this house***"* (Luke 19:9). If the person for whom you are praying is a blood relative—even a distant relative—or married to one, claim this verse for him/her.

Declarations of Salvation for Others

- God is not willing that _____ perish, but that he/she will come to repentance. (See 2 Peter 3:9.)
- God desires _____ to be saved and to come to the knowledge of the truth. (See 1 Timothy 2:4.)

- This is the confidence that I have in Him, that if I ask anything according to His will, He hears me. And I know that if (since!) He hears me, whatever I ask, I know that I have the petitions that I have asked of Him. I ask for _____ to be saved, to come to repentance, and to come to the knowledge of the truth that can set him/her free. (See 1 John 5:14–15.)

- I realize that I am not in a battle with flesh and blood, but I am contending against demonic powers, wicked spirits in the heavenly sphere, who are trying to influence and control _____. (See Ephesians 6:12.) Jesus said in Luke 10:19, *"I give you authority and power over all the power of the enemy...."*

- I agree with God's Word which says that whatever I bind on earth is bound in the heavenly sphere, where all demonic activity takes place, and that whatever I loose on earth is loosed in that same heavenly sphere. (See Matthew 18:18.) Right now, I bind the god of this world, satan, who has blinded _____'s eyes to the truth of the gospel, and I loose the light of the gospel to shine on _____ and open his/her eyes. (See 2 Corinthians 4:3–4.)

- I pray that the eyes of _____'s understanding will be opened to know the hope of his calling. (See Ephesians 1:18.) Lord, open his/her eyes to know You; open his/her understanding so that he/she may understand the Scriptures. (See Luke 24:31, 45.)

- I pray for laborers to be sent into _____'s path from the Lord of the harvest. (See Matthew 9:37–38.)

REPENTANCE

When you've stumbled and sinned, simply repent and immediately get back into fellowship with God.

Prayer of Repentance

Lord God, thank You for Your promise in Jeremiah 30:17 to restore those who fall. Thank You for granting repentance to me (see 2 Timothy 2:25), forgiving me of my sins, and for cleansing me of all unrighteousness. (See 1 John 1:9.)

Because You have granted me forgiveness to me, I know that now there is no condemnation in my life. I choose to walk in Your Spirit, Father, rather than walking after the flesh. (See Romans 8:1–2.) I now realize that to be spiritually minded is life and peace, but to be carnally minded is death. (See Romans 8:6.) Father, I want to be spiritually minded at all times.

As You remove the junk from my life, Lord, I will become a vessel for the things of the Lord. With Your help, I will speak the truth in love and, in so doing, will grow up in all things. (See Ephesians 4:15.) Thank You for Your goodness, which leads me to repentance. Because of Your goodness to me, Lord, I now repent of the following sins: _____. Thank You, Father; thank You, Jesus! Amen.

TITHES AND OFFERINGS

If you rob God of tithes and offerings, you are the loser in the long run. God is simply looking for your obedience; if you'll submit your finances to Him, you will most likely submit other areas of your life.

Besides, not paying our tithes can open a door for the enemy to come into our affairs. Proverbs 26:2 says, "*So a curse without cause shall not alight.*" In other words, there is usually a reason why the enemy thinks he has a right to come in and tear things up.

Paying your tithes and giving your offerings are the only scriptural ways of prompting God to fulfill His promise to *"open for you the windows of heaven"* (Malachi 3:10).

Tither's Confession

- I sow my tithes and offerings as a form of worship to my God.
- I sow with a heart that is thankful for God's goodness.
- I sow with a heart that is obedient to God's command.
- I declare by faith that God is providing abundantly for my future, increasing my financial status, and setting me up for success!
- I release the provision of heaven, in Jesus' name!
- I bind the enemy in the area of my finances, and declare he will not devour my blessings.
- I release the ministering angels to cause His Word to come to pass in my life.
- By faith, I declare that I am so blessed that I have finances to meet all my needs, and then abundance left over to meet the needs of others and to further the gospel!
- I am blessed coming in and blessed going out, and I prosper in everything I do!

Prayer of Provision Based on Malachi 3:8–12

Heavenly Father, I have obeyed Your Word to bring the tithes and offerings into Your house so that there may be provision in Your house. Therefore, I decree and declare Your covenant promises over my household this day.

Because we are obedient, my family and I expect these things to take place:

- We confess that the windows of heaven are being opened.
- Blessings are being poured out—there's not enough room to receive them! Surely we will shout, "It is enough! It is enough!"
- God Himself has rebuked the devourer for our sakes.
- The fruit of our ground will not be destroyed.
- Our vine won't cast its fruit before the time.
- Nations will call us blessed.
- We will be a delightful land.
- Today we are experiencing God's supernatural increase, and we walk in it by faith. We call it done, in Jesus' name. Amen.

Prayer to Anoint an Offering

Lay your hands on your seed and say:

By faith I release the love of God on and through this seed, in Jesus' name. Lord God, I love You with all my heart, all my soul, and all my mind, and all my strength; and I love my neighbor as myself. The chains of lack cannot remain under the divine pressure of obedience to the Great Commandment to love one another.

I live in the blessing of Jesus! I give this seed by faith, thanking You that I am blessed to be a blessing to others! In Jesus' name, amen.

PRAY THE WORD OF GOD

Praying the Word of God over yourself and others is powerful—it brings results, and the Bible backs this fact.

This is the confidence that we have in Him, that if we ask anything according to His will, He hears us. And if [since] we know that He hears us, whatever we ask, we know that we have the petitions that we have asked of Him.

(1 John 5:14–15)

If we ask anything according to the will of God—and His Word is certainly His will—then we can have what we ask. Therefore, in praying for yourself or others to grow spiritually, you might offer such prayers as the following.

Prayer for Spiritual Growth

Father, according to Ephesians 1:16–21, I ask and claim the Spirit of wisdom and revelation of Jesus Christ, so that we might grow in the knowledge of God. I pray that our hearts will be flooded with light (revelation knowledge) so that we can understand the wonderful future He has promised to us. I pray that we would realize what a rich and glorious inheritance He has given to us and that we would begin to understand the incredible greatness of His power for us who believe Him, because this is the same mighty power that raised Christ from the dead and seated Him in the place of honor at God's right hand in heaven. Grant us understanding that He is far above any ruler, authority, power, leader, or anything else in this world or in the world to come.

According to Ephesians 3:17–20, I ask and claim that from His glorious, unlimited resources, God will give us mighty inner strength through His Holy Spirit. And I pray that Christ will be more and more at home in our hearts, as we trust in Him. May our roots go down deep into the soil of God's marvelous love. May we have the power to understand, as all God's people should, how wide, how long, how high, and how deep His love really is. May we experience the love of Christ, though it is so great that we will never fully understand it. Then, we will be filled with the fullness of life and power that comes from God—all His blessings, resources, and wisdom. Now, glory be to God! Because of His mighty power at work within us, He is able to accomplish infinitely more than we would ever dare to ask or hope.

According to Colossians 1:9–11, I ask and claim that God will give us complete understanding of what He wants to do in our lives, and I ask Him to make us wise with spiritual wisdom. Then, the way we live will always honor and please the Lord, and we will continually do good and kind things for others. All the while, we will get to know God better and better—that is, we will become more intimately acquainted with the Father.

According to Philippians 1:9–11, I ask and claim that our love for each other will overflow more and more, and that we will keep on growing in knowledge and understanding. For I want us to understand what really matters, so that we may live pure and blameless lives until Christ returns. I pray that we may always be filled with the fruit of our salvation—those good things that are produced in our lives by Jesus Christ—for this will bring much glory and praise to God.

According to 2 Thessalonians 1:11–12, I continue to ask and claim that our God will make us worthy of the life to which He called us. And I pray that God, by His power, will fulfill all our good intentions and faithful deeds.

Then, everyone will give honor to the name of our Lord Jesus because of us; and we will be honored along with Him. This is all made possible because of the undeserved favor of our God and Lord, Jesus Christ.

According to 1 Thessalonians 5:23–24, I ask and claim that the God of peace will sanctify and makes us holy in every way, and that our whole spirit, soul, and body will be kept blameless until that day when our Lord Jesus Christ comes again. I am thankful that God, who calls us, is faithful; He will do this! In Jesus' name I pray, amen.

BAPTISM IN THE HOLY SPIRIT

"We need the baptism in the Holy Spirit so we can hear His voice saying 'Do not do this.' 'Stay away from that place today.' Instructions like these can lengthen our lives."
—Gloria Copeland

Being baptized in the Holy Spirit with the evidence of speaking with tongues is so vital for intimacy with God, and it's crucial to blasting the devil. Praying in your prayer language daily is essential to living a victorious life!

Jesus tells us that one of the signs that would distinguish His followers would be that they would pray in tongues. *"These signs **will** follow those who believe: In My name…they will speak with new tongues"* (Mark 16:17). Furthermore, the Bible shows us that the 120 people in the upper room at Pentecost (see Acts 1–2) were already saved, had been water baptized and had received the Holy Spirit as Jesus breathed on them and said *"Receive the Holy Spirit"* (John 20:22). Receiving the baptism in the Holy Spirit is a definite experience in addition to salvation, water baptism, and having the Holy Spirit come in and live in us when we are born again.

When a believer receives the baptism in the Holy Spirit, he receives a beautiful gift from the Holy Spirit—an ability to pray, to communicate with God, in a Holy Spirit-inspired language that he has never learned. *"They were all filled with the Holy Spirit and began to speak with other tongues, as the Spirit gave them utterance* [sound]" (Acts 2:4).

The Bible says that no one should ever forbid a believer from speaking in tongues. *"Brethren, desire earnestly to prophesy, and do not forbid to speak with tongues"* (1 Corinthians 14:39).

There are many, many benefits to praying in your prayer language! Why not take advantage of every weapon the Father has given you, in order to have an advantage over the enemy?

You can ask the Lord to fill you with His Spirit by praying something like the following.

Prayer for Baptism in the Holy Spirit

> Heavenly Father, You promise to give the Holy Spirit to those who ask. You say we should be filled with the Spirit; so, Lord, I ask now that You would baptize me with Your Holy Spirit, with the evidence of speaking in tongues. I pray that rivers of living water will flow from within, in the name of Jesus. I believe I receive this baptism by faith now.

What Next?

After you have asked the Lord for the baptism in the Holy Spirit, then take a deep breath and, in faith, breathe out, allowing sound to come out of your mouth. (Consider starting with "aah"—you should not make "noise" in a language you know.)

Close your eyes and picture Jesus in your mind. Think of all the wonderful things He has done for you, and then worship Him! Believe that the Holy Spirit is now helping you to give glory to almighty God as you begin to praise Him in your new heavenly prayer language!

The Scriptures tell us that we speak in tongues as the Holy Spirit gives us the ability, and that the Holy Spirit prays *with* our spirit. So, after we have prayed in a language which we know and asked Him to fill us with His Spirit, then, in faith, we must allow sound to come out of our mouths, so that the Holy Spirit can form the new prayer language we will be speaking. (There is absolutely no way you can speak in tongues if you don't allow some sound to come out of your mouth).

Once you have received the baptism in the Holy Spirit and your new prayer language (tongues), you can start or stop praying as you wish. Anytime you want to pray in this manner, the Holy Spirit will be right there to give you the utterance. Once you have received the baptism, I suggest that you just keep on praying in tongues for quite some time. It is a wonderful experience—one that you can have as often as you like each day.

Use this precious gift every day to glorify God, to build you up in the faith, and to intercede for others.

Ten Things the Holy Spirit Taught Me

1. There is a price to pay for a proper relationship with God, and the price is high—but that closeness is the most valuable possession that any human may obtain. (See Matthew 16:24–28; Mark 8:34.)

2. It is our assignment to seek God in an aggressive and dedicated manner. If we do this, God will honor and reward us. (See Hebrews 11:6.)

3. There is a devil—an enemy whose sole objective is to cause you as much grief as he can. It is up to you to make sure he doesn't achieve his goal. (See Luke 10:19.)

4. Through the resurrection of Jesus, we have been given power over the enemy. It is ours to possess and exercise. (See James 4:7.)

5. We are here for a purpose, and that purpose is to do the work of God, especially in our relationships with those God sends our way. (See Ephesians 2:10.)

6. Fear is the number one reason Christians fail to achieve their spiritual destiny. Fear is of the devil, and we have power over that low-down scoundrel. (See 2 Timothy 1:7.)

7. If you aren't full of love, you aren't where you should be with God. Simple, but totally and absolutely true. (See 1 Corinthians 13:1–13.)

8. There is definitely a baptism of the Holy Spirit, and this is the process by which power is bestowed upon the believer. (See Acts 1:8.)

9. Tongues are a definite part of the Christian life God has laid out for us. (See 1 Corinthians 14:5, 18, 22.)

10. There is a world-shaking, life-changing, godly power available to anyone who will believe and utilize that power. (See Ephesians 1:15–21; 3:14–21.)

SOWING AND REAPING

We learned many years ago from John Osteen that every time you speak the Word of God, you are "planting seeds." You need to plant spiritual seeds that will give you the harvest you desire.

So then, how do we get the faith to receive the harvest? Gloria Copeland explains it this way:

> Romans 10:17 tells us that faith comes to us by hearing God's Word, by getting it into our eyes and our ears, by getting it into our hearts, by speaking what His Word promises and by doing what it says. As we receive the Word, it begins to abide in us—it takes up residence in our hearts and lives. It becomes our existence and our way of life. We begin to totally depend on the Word as our source for everyday living.[50]

What do you need today? Do you need healing in your body? Do you need to get out of debt? Maybe you need deliverance from harmful habits, or you're asking God to mend a broken relationship. Whatever it is you need, God has the answer. It's right there in His Word."

The ultimate question is, *what is it that you want from God?*

---

50. Gloria Copeland, "Count on the Word," *Believer's Voice of Victory* (November 2010), 29.

SEEDS TO SOW IF YOU WANT TO REAP...

Healing

- "I will take sickness away from the midst of you....I will fulfill the number of your days" (Exodus 23:25–26).
- "[Jesus] forgives all your iniquities [and] heals all your diseases" (Psalm 103:1–3).
- "Surely He has borne our griefs...and carried our sorrows and pains...and with the stripes [that wounded] Him we are healed" (Isaiah 53:4 AMP).
- "He...healed all who were sick, that it might be fulfilled which was spoken by Isaiah the prophet, saying: 'He Himself took our infirmities and bore our sicknesses'" (Matthew 8:16–17; see also Isaiah 53:5).
- "I am the LORD who heals you" (Exodus 15:26).
- "I shall not die, but live, and declare the works of the LORD" (Psalm 118:17).
- "He gives power to the faint and weary, and to him who has no might He increases strength....Those who wait on the Lord...shall change and renew their strength and power; they shall life their wings and mount up [close to God] as eagles [mount up to the sun]; they shall run and not be weary; they shall walk and not faint or become tired" (Isaiah 40:29, 31 AMP).

Abundant Provision

- "Beloved, I pray that you may prosper in all things and be in health, just as your soul prospers" (3 John 1:2).

- "My God shall supply all your need according to His riches in glory by Christ Jesus" (Philippians 4:19).

- "Praise the LORD! Blessed is the man who fears the LORD, who delights greatly in His commandments. His descendants will be mighty on earth; the generation of the upright will be blessed. Wealth and riches will be in his house, and his righteousness endures forever" (Psalm 112:1–3).

- "They that seek the LORD shall not want any good thing" (Psalm 34:10 KJV).

- "The Lord is my Shepherd [to feed, guide, and shield me], I shall not lack" (Psalm 23:1 AMP).

- Make this your personal confession: "I trust (lean on, rely on and am confident) in the Lord, and I do good; therefore, I shall dwell in the land and surely feed on His faithfulness, and truly I will be fed! I delight myself in the Lord, and He will give me the desires and secret petitions of my heart. I commit my way to the Lord. I roll each care of my load on Him. I trust (lean on, rely on and am confident) in Him, and He will bring it to pass." (See Psalm 37:3–5 AMP.)

Miracles

- "Now this is the confidence that we have in Him, that if we ask anything according to His will, He hears us. And if [since!] we know that He hears us, whatever we ask, we know that we have the petitions that we have asked of Him" (1 John 5:14–15).

- "For assuredly, I say to you, whoever says to this mountain, 'Be removed and be cast into the sea,' and does not doubt in his heart, but believes that those things he says will be done, he will have whatever he says. Therefore I say to you, whatever things you ask when you pray, believe that you receive them, and you will have them" (Mark 11:23–24).

- "Today salvation [deliverance, preservation, soundness, prosperity, happiness, rescue, and well-being] *has come to this house*" (Luke 19:9).

- "*No weapon formed against you shall prosper*" (Isaiah 54:17).

Divine Direction and Guidance

- "*Call to Me and I will answer you and show you great and mighty things…which you do not know*" (Jeremiah 33:3 AMP)

- "*[I] have an anointing from the Holy One, and [I] know all things*" (1 John 2:20).

- "*I will instruct you and teach you in the way you should go; I will guide you with My eye*" (Psalm 32:8).

- "We follow the Good Shepherd and know His voice. We will not follow the voice of a stranger." (See John 10:4–5.)

Boldness Instead of Fear

- "*For He Himself has said, 'I will never leave you nor forsake you.' So we may boldly say: 'The LORD is my helper; I will not fear. What can man do to me?'*" (Hebrews 13:6).

- "*Fear not [there is nothing to fear], for I am with you; do not look around you in terror and be dismayed, for I am your God. I will strengthen and harden you to difficulties, yes, I will help you; yes, I will hold you up and retain you with My [victorious] right hand of rightness and justice*" (Isaiah 41:10 AMP).

- "The LORD is my rock, and my fortress, and my deliverer; my God, my strength, in whom I will trust; my buckler, and the horn of my salvation, and my high tower" (Psalm 18:2 KJV).
- "Though I walk through the valley of the shadow of death, I will fear no evil" (Psalm 23:4).
- "Though an army may encamp against me, my heart shall not fear" (Psalm 27:3).
- "God is our refuge and strength, a very present help in trouble. Therefore we will not fear, even though the earth be removed, and though the mountains be carried into the midst of the sea" (Psalm 46:1–2).

The Peace of Protection and Safety

- No harm or grave trouble will befall me, because I am righteous in Christ. (See Proverbs 12:21.)
- I will both lie down in peace and sleep, for the Lord alone makes me dwell in safety. (See Psalm 4:8.)
- God is my strong refuge to whom I continually resort. (See Psalm 71:3.)
- "I will not be afraid of ten thousands of people who have set themselves against me all around" (Psalm 3:6).
- God surrounds me with a shield of favor. (See Psalm 5:12.)
- God has given me authority to trample on snakes and scorpions and to overcome all the power of the enemy; nothing will harm me! (See Luke 10:19.)
- I dwell in the shelter of the Most High and rest in the shadow of the Almighty. The Lord is my refuge and my fortress; my God in whom I trust. (See Psalm 91:1–2.)

- He will cover me with His feathers, and under His wings I will find refuge. His faithfulness is my shield and protection. (See Psalm 91:4.)

- "[I] *will not fear the terror of night, nor the arrow that flies by day, nor the pestilence that stalks in the darkness, nor the plague that destroys at midday*" (Psalm 91:5–6 NIV).

- A thousand may fall at my side, even ten thousand at my right hand, but it will not come near me because I have made the Most High my dwelling place. (See Psalm 91:7, 9.)

- No harm will befall me; no disaster will come anywhere near me. (See Psalm 91:10 NIV.)

- God commands His angels concerning me. They will guard me in all my ways and keep me from stumbling. (See Psalm 91:11–12.)

- With long life God will satisfy me (see Psalm 91:16); He will deliver me from the evil one (see Matthew 6:13). He will demonstrate His salvation to me because I know His names, and I am intimately acquainted with Him.

Salvation, for Yourself or Others

- "For God so loved the world that He gave His only begotten Son, that whoever believes in Him should not perish but have everlasting life" (John 3:16).

- "*Christ died for* [the ungodly]" (Romans 5:8).

- "*All we like sheep have gone astray; we have turned, every one, to his own way; and the* LORD *has laid on* [Jesus] *the iniquity of us all*" (Isaiah 53:6).

- "Believe on the Lord Jesus Christ, and you will be saved, you and your household" (Acts 16:31).
- "As many as received him, to them gave he power to become the sons of God, even to them that believe on his name" (John 1:12 KJV).
- "Whoever calls on the name of the LORD shall be saved" (Romans 10:13).
- "If you confess with your mouth the Lord Jesus and believe in your heart that God has raised Him from the dead, you will be saved. For with the heart one believes unto righteousness, and with the mouth confession is made unto salvation" (Romans 10:9–10).

Victory over Weakness and Failure

- "Now may the God of hope fill you with all joy and peace in believing, that you may abound in hope by the power of the Holy Spirit. Now I myself am confident concerning you, my brethren, that you also are full of goodness" (Romans 15:13–14).
- "Resist the devil and he will flee from you" (James 4:7).
- "The Son of God was manifested, that He might destroy the works of the devil" (1 John 3:8).
- "Having disarmed principalities and powers, He made a public spectacle of them, triumphing over them in it" (Colossians 2:15).
- "Behold, I give you the authority to trample on serpents and scorpions, and over all the power of the enemy, and nothing shall by any means hurt you" (Luke 10:19).

The Joy of Seeing Your Children and Grandchildren Serving God

- All of my children are taught of the Lord, and great will be their peace and undisturbed composure. (See Isaiah 54:13 AMP.)
- I and the children whom the Lord has given me are signs and wonders. (See Isaiah 8:18.)
- God said His Spirit that is upon me and that His words which He has put in my mouth will not depart out of my mouth, or out of the mouth of my seed, or out of the mouth of my seed's seed. (See Isaiah 59:21.)
- As I hunger and thirst for God, He will pour His Spirit upon me and my seed and His blessings upon my offspring. They will spring up as the grass, as willows by the water courses—healthy, prosperous, and stable. (See Isaiah 44:3–4.)
- The seed of the righteous shall be delivered. (See Proverbs 11:21.)
- The Lord will contend with him who contends with me, and He will save my children. (See Isaiah 49:25.)
- Because I fear the Lord, my seed shall be mighty upon the earth. The generation of the upright shall be blessed. Since I am upright, my children and grandchildren will be blessed. (See Psalm 112:1–3.)
- Our offspring will be known among the nations, and their descendants among the peoples. All who see them will acknowledge that they are the people whom the Lord has blessed. (See Isaiah 61:9.)
- God will bless those who fear Him, both small and great. The Lord will increase us more and more, us and our children. (See Psalm 115:13–14.)

WISDOM AND GUIDANCE

"What we learn in the presence of God can never be learned in the presence of men."
—John Bevere

Proverbs 4:7 says that the most important thing is to get skillful and godly wisdom. Likewise, we must also seek true understanding to *apply* the wisdom we receive from the Holy Spirit.

Prayer for Guidance in Decision Making[51]

Father, I ask for and claim wisdom to make right decisions today. I declare that we are *"filled with the knowledge of [God's] will in all wisdom and spiritual understanding"* (Colossians 1:9).

Father, Your Word says in John 10:27 that we, Your sheep, can know Your voice. It says in John 16:13 that You will show us things to come. It says the voice of Your Spirit will come to us and say, *"This is the way, walk in it"* (Isaiah 30:21). I stand on these promises, Lord, and ask that You would teach us to hear Your voice. Help us

---

51. Parts are slightly revised from Kellie Copeland Kutz's "Prayer of Protection for Your Family." http://www.wellsofblessing.org/protectfamily.html.

recognize when You are speaking to us, and, Holy Spirit, give us the grace to obey.

Now I stand in Your Holy of Holies and open my spirit to receive the wisdom You have promised. I put myself in a position to hear and receive instructions from You. I have entered the secret place of the Most High by the blood of the Lamb, and I purpose to live my life in Your presence and always hear Your voice.

Prayer for Wisdom

Heavenly Father, I thank You that we have been granted the spirit of wisdom and revelation, and we have insight into Your ways of doing things. We will yield to the direction of the Holy Spirit for every decision we must make, because our spiritual eyes are flooded with Light. We know what to do in every situation we face; we are never lost or confused when it comes to making the right decision.

Thank You that we are filled with the knowledge of Your will for our lives, and we make wise choices. We acknowledge You before making any decisions, and we seek Your direction at all times. We are willing to stop if You tell us to stop, or to go when You tell us to go. Because we acknowledge You, You direct our footsteps, and we will remain in the perfect will of God throughout all of our lives.

Your Word is our final Authority, and every choice we make will line up with it. We will not disregard the peace of God in helping us to make decisions. We will align our lives with Your Word; therefore, we will remain connected to Your best for our lives. Thank You for giving us Your Word and Your Holy Spirit, who guides us into all Truth. In Jesus' name I pray, amen.

Declarations of Divine Wisdom and Guidance[52]

Make these faith declarations and receive His wisdom and guidance for your life:

- The Spirit of truth abides in us and teaches us all things. He guides us into all truth. Therefore, I confess that we have perfect knowledge of every situation and every circumstance that tries to come against us; for we have the wisdom of God abiding in us. (See John 16:13; James 1:5.)
- We will trust in the Lord with all our hearts and lean not on our own understanding. (See Proverbs 3:5.)
- Because we acknowledge the Lord in all our ways, He will direct our paths. (See Proverbs 3:6.)
- The Lord will perfect that which concerns us. (See Psalm 138:8.)
- We let the Word of Christ dwell in us abundantly in all wisdom. (See Colossians 3:16.)
- We follow the Good Shepherd; we know His voice, and the voice of a stranger we will not follow. (See John 10:4–5.)
- Jesus has already made available to us wisdom, righteousness, sanctification, and redemption. Therefore, I confess that we have the wisdom of God and that we are the righteousness of God in Christ Jesus. We are redeemed, we are sanctified, and walk in holiness before Him. (See 1 Corinthians 1:30; 2 Corinthians 5:21.)

---

52. Declarations adapted from Charles Capps, *God's Creative Power Will Work for You* (Tulsa, OK: Harrison House, Inc., 1976).

- We are new creations in Christ; we are His workmanship, created in Christ Jesus. Therefore, we have the mind of Christ, and the wisdom of God is formed within us. (See 2 Corinthians 5:17; Ephesians 2:10; 1 Corinthians 2:16.)
- We have received the Spirit of wisdom and revelation in the knowledge of Him; therefore, the eyes of our understanding are enlightened. We are not conformed to this world, but we are transformed by the renewing of our minds, which happens through the Word of God. (See Ephesians 1:17–18; Romans 12:2.)
- I declare that we are *"filled with the knowledge of [God's] will in all wisdom and spiritual understanding"* (Colossians 1:9).

I CAN KNOW ALL THINGS

We *can* know the will of God for our lives! We *can* know what to do in every situation; God is not trying to hide anything from us. Declaring these Scriptures regularly, in faith, invites the guidance of the Holy Spirit in all of our affairs.

Scriptural Confessions of Knowing All Things

- I have an unction from the Holy One; therefore, I can know all things. (See 1 John 2:20.)
- Jesus has made known to me all that He has heard from His Father. (See John 15:15.)
- The Lord does nothing unless He reveals His secrets to His servants. I am a servant of God; therefore, I have His wisdom and revelation knowledge. (See Amos 3:7.)
- The Holy Spirit reveals the deep and secret things to me. I know what is in the darkness, and the light dwells within me. (See Daniel 2:22.)

- I believe what Jesus said—that there is nothing hidden that will not be revealed, and there is nothing secret that will not come to light. (See Mark 4:22.)
- God has promised to grant me full insight and understanding in all things. (See 2 Timothy 2:7.)
- Because I seek the Lord, I understand all things. (See Proverbs 28:5.)
- Anything I have lost, I will find, because God has promised that if I ask, it will be given to me; that if I seek, I will find. (See Matthew 7:7.)

WORSHIP

Richard Foster has said, "Adoration is the spontaneous yearning of the heart to worship, honor, magnify, and bless God. We ask for nothing—only to cherish Him. We seek nothing but His exaltation. We focus on nothing but His goodness. In the prayer of adoration we love God for Himself, for His very being.

"When I give thanks, my thoughts still circle about myself to some extent. But in praise, my soul ascends to adoration, entirely forgetting about myself, and seeing and praising only the majesty and power of God, His grace and redemption."[53]

Prayer to Bless the Names of God[54]

- *Elohim*

  I bless *Elohim*—God, the mighty Creator.
  You are the Maker of heaven and earth.
  You have created us in Your image,
  and I magnify Your name.

- *El Shaddai*

  I bless You, *El Shaddai*—God Almighty, the God of blessings.
  You are the many-breasted One, who nourishes and

---

53. Richard J. Foster, *Prayer: Finding the Hearts True Home*, 10th Anniversary Edition (New York: HarperCollins Publishers, 1992, 1995), 81.
54. Concept adapted from Germaine Copeland, *Prayers That Avail Much* (Tulsa, OK: Harrison House, 1999).

supplies. (See Psalm 91:1.)
You are the God who is more than enough!
Hallowed be Your name!

- *Adonai*

  I bless You, *Adonai*—my Lord and Master.
  I am not my own. I have been bought with a price—the blood of the Lamb!
  I love You and serve You.
  My spirit, soul, and body belong to You!

- *Jehovah*

  You are *Jehovah* and the great "I Am Who I Am" (Exodus 3:14)!
  It is my joy to submit to Your good ways,
  to always follow You! I bless You!

- *Jehovah-Rohi*

  I bless *Jehovah-Rohi*—the Lord our Shepherd.
  We are Your sheep; we know Your voice.
  The voice of another we will not follow.
  Thank You, Lord, that You are the One
  who guides, feeds, and shields us.

- *Jehovah-Jireh*

  I bless You, *Jehovah-Jireh*—the Lord our Provider.
  We shall not want or lack any good thing.
  You are the One who makes provision for us.
  Thank You that Jesus was the "ram in the thicket"! (See Genesis 22:13.)

- *Jehovah-Shalom*

  I bless *Jehovah-Shalom*—the Lord is Peace.
  In You, we have provision, protection, and peace.

You are our security, our wholeness, and our well-being.
Because of You, there is "nothing missing and nothing broken" in our lives.

- *Jehovah-M'Kaddesh*

    I bless You, *Jehovah-M'Kaddesh*—the Lord our Sanctifier.
    You are the One who sanctifies us and makes us holy.
    You have set us apart for Yourself.
    Hallowed be Your name!

- *Jehovah-Tsidkenu*

    Blessed be *Jehovah-Tsidkenu*—the Lord our Righteousness.
    Because of the blood of Jesus, we are in right standing with You.
    I honor You for Your blood today!

- *Jehovah-Shammah*

    Hallelujah to *Jehovah-Shammah*—the Lord is there.
    You will never leave us nor forsake us. (See Deuteronomy 31:6.)
    Thank You, Holy Spirit, for Your abiding presence.

- *Jehovah-Nissi*

    I bless You, *Jehovah-Nissi*—the Lord my Banner.
    You are our Victory, our miracle Worker.
    No enemy dares to cross the blood line!
    Hallowed be Your name!

- *Jehovah-Rapha*

    I bless You, *Jehovah-Rapha*—the Lord who heals.
    You are our Healer and the One who makes bitter experiences sweet.

You sent Your Word to heal us.
You forgave all our iniquities and You healed all our diseases.
Glory to Your name!

- *Jehovah-Sabaoth*

I bless You, *Jehovah-Sabaoth*—the Lord of hosts.
You are the God who commands angelic armies to defend and protect us.
As we speak Your Word in faith, Your angels see to it that it is fulfilled.
Blessed be the name of the Lord!

- *El Elyon*

I worship and adore You, *El Elyon*—the Most High God.
I praise the Most High, whose power, mercy, and sovereignty cannot be matched.
I bless the Most High, and I honor the One who lives forever!
Hallowed be Your names!

	Psalm 23: A Guide for Praise and Worship Using the Redemptive Names of Jehovah		
Verse	Our Father has many, many names in the Hebrew Bible—some say as many as 144—each revealing a different aspect of His greatness and power. Nearly every phrase in Psalm 23 represents a *redemptive name* of Jehovah—describing at least nine important benefits that Jesus purchased for us on the cross. These names help us better understand His protection and provision for us. As you pray Psalm 23 back to Him, bless the Lord using these names. If you have only a short amount of time available to spend with the Lord, this guide covers all the bases and helps you get into the presence of God.		"I BLESS YOU…"
Verse 1	*"The LORD is my shepherd."* Lord, according to John 10:14, You are our Good Shepherd, and we are Your sheep; we know Your voice, and the voice of another we will not follow. I stand against a spirit of deception and a lying spirit in every member of my immediate and extended family and in my church. Thank You, Lord, that You are the One who guides, feeds, and shields us. I bless You.	*Jehovah-Rohi* The Lord our Shepherd
	"I shall not want." Thank You, Lord, that according to Philippians 4:9, You supply all of our need. You are the *"I AM WHO I AM"* (Exodus 3:14)—the Provider of everything we need, in spirit, soul, and body. *Jehovah-Jireh* is the One who will see to it that our every need is met. Father, You are everything we will ever need. I receive You today as…	*Jehovah-Jireh* The Lord our Provider, The Lord who sees

Verse 2	*"He makes me to lie down in green pastures."* Lord, thank You for Your provision, protection, and peace. Because You are our *Jehovah-Shalom*, we can live life at its best! Thank You for wholeness and security.	
	"He leads me beside the still waters." You are the God of Peace. Thank You for wholeness, rest, and safety. Isaiah 26:3 says that You will keep us in perfect peace if we keep our mind on You and trust in You. We are determined to live a stress-free life because Jesus said in John 14:27, *"Peace I leave with you, My peace I give to you.... Let not your heart be troubled, neither let it be afraid."* We agree with the Word in Philippians 4:6–7, which says that *"the peace of God, which surpasses all understanding, shall guard our hearts and minds through Christ Jesus."* Thank You for being...	*Jehovah-Shalom* The Lord our Peace
Verse 3	*"He restores my soul."* Lord God, as our Great Physician, You not only heal our bodies; You also heal all the hurts in our soul—our mind, will, and emotions. You heal the brokenhearted. (See Psalm 147:3.) As our Sanctifier, You are the One who keeps us holy. We will not be conformed to this world; rather, we will be transformed (set apart) by the renewing of our minds. (See Romans 12:1–2.) I declare and claim that Your Word will continually renew our minds. The only way our souls can be restored is through the Word of God, so I bind our minds to the mind of Christ and our will to the will of God. I bless...	*Jehovah-Rapha* The Lord who heals
	"He leads me in the paths of righteousness for His name's sake." Psalm 37:23 says that *"the steps of a good man are directed by the Lord."* Thank You, Father, that the Holy Spirit leads us in the right direction, not because we have earned it, but because of His great love for us, and also because of the integrity of the Word of God. I bind our feet to the paths of righteousness that You have ordained for us to walk. Father, thank You for the blood of Jesus. It is the blood that makes us in right standing with You. I honor the blood today, and bless You as...	*Jehovah-M'Kaddesh* The Lord our Sanctifier

Verse 4	*"Though I walk through the valley of the shadow of death, I will fear no evil; for You are with me."* Thank You for Your abiding presence, Holy Spirit. Thank You that You are here, fellowshipping with me. I welcome You, Holy Spirit. No matter where we are, *Jehovah-Shammah* is there! He will never leave us, because His presence is within us. Lord, You said in Psalm 66:12 that we went through fire and through water, but You brought us out into a large place of wealth and abundance. Nothing missing, nothing broken! Second Timothy 1:7 says that *"God has not given us a spirit of fear, but of power and of love and of a sound mind."* We will not be afraid, because You are always with us. The shadow of a dog never bit anyone! I bless…	**Jehovah-Shammah** *The Lord is there*
	"Your rod and Your staff, they comfort me." Father, I receive Your comfort and guidance today; thank You for delivering us! Thank You for Your precious Holy Spirit and Your Word. (The rod in this verse represents the Holy Spirit—our Guide, Comforter, and Helper. The staff represents the Word of God in power: the club part of the rod is used against the sheep's enemies, and the crook/shaft is used to rescue the sheep.)	**Thank You for the Holy Spirit and the Word of God!**
Verse 5	*"You prepare a table before me in the presence of my enemies."* Thank You, Lord, that as *Jehovah-Nissi*, You promote us and declare us champions over our enemies, even during times of great conflict and war. *"When the enemy comes in like a flood, the Spirit of the LORD will lift up a standard [banner] against him"* (Isaiah 59:19). Even if it seems like the whole camp of the enemy is thrown at us, we remember that Christ died and triumphed over death, then rose from the grave with the keys of life and death in His hands. We are the friends of God, and *Jehovah-Nissi* is our Banner—a banner of love and protection. (See Song of Solomon 2:4.) *"Thanks be to God, who gives us the victory through our Lord Jesus Christ"* (1 Corinthians 15:57). Thank You, Lord, for being our victory in every situation! I bless You as…	**Jehovah-Nissi** *The Lord our Banner,* *The Lord of Victory,* *Our Miracle Worker*

A "table" was an area the shepherd sectioned off for a sick or crippled sheep. He laid his cloak on one side, his rod on another side, his staff on another side; finally, he himself lay down on the fourth side. These items created a barrier which no enemy dared to cross. The Lord revealed to me that these items represent the Holy Spirit, the Word of God, the name of Jesus, and the blood of Jesus, all of which surround us and protect us. *The enemy dare not cross the blood line!*

Verse 5	*"You anoint my head with oil."* You are God our Healer. By Your stripes, we are healed. (See Isaiah 53:5.) Thank You, Lord, that we are healed because of the wounds Jesus took for us. We remember James' instruction to pray for the sick: *"Is anyone among you sick? Let him call for the elders of the church, and let them pray over him, anointing him with oil in the name of the Lord"* (James 5:14). I declare that You are *Jehovah-Rapha* today, and I bless You as…	*Jehovah-Rapha* The Lord who heals
	"My cup runs over." You are *El Shaddai*—the God who is more than enough! Your Word says that according to Your power that works in us, You are able to accomplish infinitely more than we would ever ask or think. (See Ephesians 3:20.) Thank You for overflow in every area of our lives! I receive You as…	*El Shaddai* Almighty God
Verse 6	*"Surely goodness and mercy shall follow me all the days of my life; and I will dwell in the house of the* LORD *forever."* Thank You, Lord, for Your unending goodness and mercy toward us (see Psalm 100:5), for You are good, and Your unfailing love continues forever (see Psalm 118:1–4 NIV). Thank You that You have gone to prepare a mansion for us. (See John 14:2.) We will spend all of eternity with You! Hallelujah! I bless…	*Adonai* My Lord and Master

And now, all glory be to God, who is able to keep us from stumbling and who will bring us into His glorious presence, innocent and joyful. All glory to Him, who alone is God our Savior, through Jesus Christ our Lord. Yes, all glory, majesty, power, and authority belong to Him, as it was in the beginning, as it is now, and as it shall be forevermore. (See Jude 1:24–25.) Jesus, be magnified in every area of our lives! Amen!

Scriptures and Scriptural Declarations to Exalt the Lord

- "I will love the Lord my God with all my heart, all my soul, and all my strength." (See Matthew 22:37.)

- I will sing of Your strength; in the morning I will sing of Your love, for You are our fortress, our refuge in times of trouble, and our Strength. I sing praises to You; O God, You are our defense, our loving God. (See Psalm 59:16–17.)

- I will love You fervently and devotedly, O Lord, my strength. The Lord is our rock, our fortress, and our deliverer. You are our God, our strength, in whom we will trust and take refuge; our shield and the horn of our salvation, our high tower. I will call upon the Lord who is greatly to be praised, and so will we be saved from our enemies. (See Psalm 18:1–3.)

- "I will extol You, my God, O King; and I will bless Your name forever and ever [with grateful, affectionate praise]. Every day [with its new reasons] will I bless You [affectionately and gratefully praise You]; yes, I will praise Your name forever and ever. Great is the Lord and highly to be praised; and His greatness is [so vast and deep as to be] unsearchable" (Psalm 145:1–3 AMP).

- "The Lord lives! Blessed be my Rock; and let the God of my salvation be exalted" (Psalm 18:46 AMP).

- "Be exalted, O God, above the heavens! Let Your glory be over all the earth!...My heart is fixed, O God, my heart is steadfast and confident! I will sing and make melody....I will praise and give thanks to You, O Lord, among the peoples; I will sing praises to You among the nations. For Your mercy and loving-kindness are great, reaching to the heavens, and Your truth and faithfulness to the clouds. Be exalted, O God, above the heavens; let Your glory be over all the earth" (Psalm 57:5–11 AMP).

- O God, my heart is fixed (committed and unwavering). I will sing and give praise to You. I will praise You, Lord, among the people, and I will sing praises unto You among the nations, because Your mercy is great above the heavens and Your truth reaches to the clouds. Be exalted, O God, above the heavens, and let Your glory shine above all the earth. (See Psalm 108:1–5.)

- "Be exalted, O LORD, in Your own strength! We will sing and praise Your power" (Psalm 21:13 AMP).
- "[I] extol the Lord our God and worship at His holy hill, for the Lord our God is holy!" (Psalm 99:9 AMP).
- "You are my God, and I will confess, praise, and give thanks to You; You are my God, I will extol You" (Psalm 118:28 AMP).
- "Lord, You are my God; I will exalt You, I will praise Your name, for You have done wonderful things, even purposes planned of old [and fulfilled] in faithfulness and truth" (Isaiah 25:1 AMP).
- I will bless the Most High and praise and honor the One who lives forever, for His sovereignty is an everlasting sovereignty, and His kingdom endures from generation to generation. His works are all faithful and right, and His ways are just. (See Daniel 4:34, 37 AMP.)
- "Blessed be the Lord, my Rock and my keen and firm Strength...my Steadfast Love and my Fortress, my High Tower and my Deliverer, my Shield and He in Whom I trust and take refuge, Who subdues my people under me" (Psalm 144:1–2 AMP).
- "Worthy is the Lamb... to receive power and riches

> "THE DEPTH OF YOUR PRAISE WILL DETERMINE THE MAGNITUDE OF YOUR BREAKTHROUGH."
> —JERRY SAVELLE

and wisdom, and strength and honor and glory and blessing!" (Revelation 5:12).

ABOUT THE AUTHOR

Gail Winter—author, teacher, and speaker—is passionate about teaching people how to be overcomers in every situation. Gail was born and raised in a wonderful Christian family on a farm in South Dakota. She graduated from Central Christian College, a two-year college in McPherson, Kansas, with a degree in general studies. At the recommendation of a professor, she continued her education at Greenville College in Illinois, where she earned a B.S. in business education. Her education has given her the background necessary to do the things that God has called her to do. Gail has been an entrepreneur and business owner for more than thirty years. Presently, she owns an office supply and furniture business, in addition to managing Speak His Word Ministries, which she and her husband, Raymond, founded in 2009. Gail is a licensed and ordained minister and has been teaching the Word of God for more than twenty-five years. With their three children grown, married, and serving God, Gail and Raymond now live in Borger, Texas.

Welcome to Our House!
We Have a Special Gift for You

It is our privilege and pleasure to share in your love of Christian books. We are committed to bringing you authors and books that feed, challenge, and enrich your faith.

To show our appreciation, we invite you sign up to receive a specially selected **Reader Appreciation Gift**, with our compliments. Just go to the Web address at the bottom of this page.

God bless you as you seek a deeper walk with Him!

WE HAVE A GIFT FOR YOU. VISIT:

whpub.me/nonfictionthx

WHITAKER HOUSE